Smoking

Editor: Danielle Lobban

Volume 406

First published by Independence Educational Publishers

The Studio, High Green

Great Shelford

Cambridge CB22 5EG

England

© Independence 2022

Copyright

This book is sold subject to the condition that it shall not, by way of trade or otherwise, be lent, resold, hired out or otherwise circulated in any form of binding or cover other than that in which it is published without the publisher's prior consent.

Photocopy licence

The material in this book is protected by copyright. However, the purchaser is free to make multiple copies of particular articles for instructional purposes for immediate use within the purchasing institution. Making copies of the entire book is not permitted.

ISBN-13: 978 1 86168 865 1

Printed in Great Britain

Zenith Print Group

Contents

Chapter 1: Smoking Overview

Number of smokers has reached all-time high of 1.1 billion, study finds	1
Smoking costs society £17 billion – £5 billion more than previously estimated	2
A third of smoking households in England are living in poverty with rates highest in the North	4
Lockdown reverses 40-year decline in smoking	6
Smoking-related cancer twice as prevalent among poor in England	7
Nicotine addiction & side effects on the body	8
Silent sleep danger for smokers uncovered in world-first study	12
Second-hand smoke: when you work in others' homes, where do their rights end and yours begin?	14

Chapter 2: E-cigarettes & Vaping

8 things to know about e-cigarettes	16
Vaping better than nicotine replacement therapy for stopping smoking, evidence suggests	18
Vape users warned about potential explosions or fire if they use wrong batteries	20
WHO warning on vaping draws harsh response from UK researchers	21
A damning review of e-cigarettes shows vaping leads to smoking, the opposite of what supporters claim	22
E-cigarettes could be prescribed on the NHS in world first	24

Chapter 3: Quitting

The benefits of stopping smoking	25
Quitting smoking is linked to improved mental health, research finds	26
Smoking and pregnancy: financial incentives can double abstinence rates	28
Smoke-free England by 2030: On track or unrealistic?	30
Stop smoking treatments	32
Smoking banned in beer gardens by five councils across England	34
Countries share examples of how tobacco tax policies create win-wins for development, health and revenues	35
Age restriction for buying cigarettes could be changed under new plan	37
How to help a friend quit smoking	38

Key Facts	40
Glossary	41
Activities	42
Index	43
Acknowledgements	44

Introduction

Smoking is Volume 406 in the **issues** series. The aim of the series is to offer current, diverse information about important issues in our world, from a UK perspective.

About Smoking

Despite the well-known serious health risks, a recent study found there are still over 1 billion smokers worldwide. In the UK, a 40-year decline in the habit has been put into reverse as a result of increased stress during the pandemic. This book looks at the addictive qualities and effects of smoking and considers the increasing and controversial use of e-cigarettes and vaping. It also explores incentives to quit the habit for good.

OUR SOURCES

Titles in the **issues** series are designed to function as educational resource books, providing a balanced overview of a specific subject.

The information in our books is comprised of facts, articles and opinions from many different sources, including:

- Newspaper reports and opinion pieces
- Website factsheets
- Magazine and journal articles
- Statistics and surveys
- Government reports
- Literature from special interest groups.

A NOTE ON CRITICAL EVALUATION

Because the information reprinted here is from a number of different sources, readers should bear in mind the origin of the text and whether the source is likely to have a particular bias when presenting information (or when conducting their research). It is hoped that, as you read about the many aspects of the issues explored in this book, you will critically evaluate the information presented.

It is important that you decide whether you are being presented with facts or opinions. Does the writer give a biased or unbiased report? If an opinion is being expressed, do you agree with the writer? Is there potential bias to the 'facts' or statistics behind an article?

ASSIGNMENTS

In the back of this book, you will find a selection of assignments designed to help you engage with the articles you have been reading and to explore your own opinions. Some tasks will take longer than others and there is a mixture of design, writing and research-based activities that you can complete alone or in a group.

FURTHER RESEARCH

At the end of each article we have listed its source and a website that you can visit if you would like to conduct your own research. Please remember to critically evaluate any sources that you consult and consider whether the information you are viewing is accurate and unbiased.

Useful Websites

www.allencarr.com

www.ash.org.uk

www.birmingham.ac.uk

www.gov.uk

www.hriuk.org

www.independent.co.uk

www.lordslibrary.parliament.uk

www.metro.co.uk

www.more-life.co.uk

www.nhs.uk

www.science.org

www.telegraph.co.uk

www.theconversation.com

www.theguardian.co.uk

www.ukhsa.blog.gov.uk

www.who.int

Chapter 1: Smoking Overview

Number of smokers has reached all-time high of 1.1 billion, study finds

Governments told to focus on stopping young from taking up habit that killed 8 million people in 2019.

By Kaamil Ahmed

Smoking killed almost 8 million people in 2019 and the number of smokers rose as the habit was picked up by young people around the world, according to new research.

A study published in the Lancet on Thursday said efforts to curb the habit had been outstripped by population growth with 150 million more people smoking in the nine years from 1990, reaching an all-time high of 1.1 billion.

The study's authors said governments need to focus on reducing the uptake of smoking among young people, as 89% of new smokers were addicted by the age of 25 but beyond that age were unlikely to start.

'Young people are particularly vulnerable to addiction, and with high rates of cessation remaining elusive worldwide, the tobacco epidemic will continue for years to come unless countries can dramatically reduce the number of new smokers starting each year,' said the study's lead author Marissa Reitsma, a researcher at the Institute for Health Metrics and Evaluation.

Though the prevalence of smoking has reduced globally over the past three decades, it increased for men in 20 countries and for women in 12. Just 10 countries made up two-thirds of the world's smoking population: China, India, Indonesia, the US, Russia, Bangladesh, Japan, Turkey, Vietnam and the Philippines. One in three tobacco smokers (341 million) live in China.

In 2019, smoking was associated with 1.7 million deaths from ischaemic heart disease, 1.6 million deaths from chronic obstructive pulmonary disease, 1.3 million deaths from tracheal, bronchus and lung cancer, and nearly 1 million deaths from stroke. Previous studies have shown that at least half of long-term smokers will die from causes directly linked to smoking, and that smokers have an average life expectancy 10 years lower than those who have never smoked.

The research examined trends in 204 countries and was produced as part of the Global Burden of Disease consortium of researchers, which studies health issues that lead to death and disability.

According to the study, half of all the countries had made no progress in stopping uptake among 15- to 24-year-olds and the average age for someone to start was 19, when it is legal in most places.

Reitsma said the evidence suggested that if young people faced delays in picking up the habit they would be less likely to end up becoming smokers at all.

'Ensuring that young people remain smoke-free through their mid-20s will result in radical reductions in smoking rates for the next generation,' said Reitsma.

Despite 182 countries signing a 2005 convention on tobacco control, enforcing policies to reduce smoking had been varied. Researchers said taxation was the most effective policy but there was a significant discrepancy between the high cost of a packet of cigarettes in developed countries and a significantly lower costs in low- and middle-income countries.

The study's co-author, Vin Gupta, said there needed to be stronger commitment to tackling smoking, as well as products such as flavoured cigarettes and e-cigarettes that could be enticing young people.

'Despite progress in some countries, tobacco industry interference and waning political commitment have resulted in a large and persistent gap between knowledge and action on global tobacco control,' said Gupta.

'Bans on advertising, promotion and sponsorship must extend to internet-based media, but only one in four countries have comprehensively banned all forms of direct and indirect advertising.'

27 May 2021

The above information is reprinted with kind permission from *The Guardian*.
© 2022 Guardian News and Media Limited

www.theguardian.com

Smoking costs society £17 billion – £5 billion more than previously estimated

New economic analysis of national data for ASH finds the cost of smoking to society is significantly higher than previous estimates have shown. Commissioned by charity Action on Smoking and Health (ASH) the new figures[1] published today [Thursday 13th January] show the cost of smoking to society totals £17.04 billion for England each year. This compares to £12.5 billion under the previous estimate[2].

The higher estimate is a result of a new assessment of the impact of smoking on productivity[3]. Smokers are more likely than non-smokers to become ill while of working age increasing the likelihood of being out of work and reducing the average wages of smokers. Smokers are also more likely to die while they are still of working age creating a further loss to the economy. Together this adds up to £13.2 billion.

Smokers' need for health and social care at a younger age than non-smokers also creates costs, with smoking costing the NHS an additional £2.4 billion and a further £1.2 billion in social care costs. This includes the cost of care provided in the home and, for the first time, residential care costs.

The costs have been broken down so local authorities and regions can see the impact of smoking in their area.

Summary data below:

Area Name	Number of smokers	Overall cost	Healthcare costs	Productivity costs	Social care costs	Fire costs
England	6,144,703	17.04 billion	2.40 billion	13.17 billion	1.19 billion	282.78 million
East midlands	568,751	1.55 billion	217.29 million	1.19 billion	118.04 million	26.56 million
East of England	670,686	1.84 billion	283.67 million	1.40 billion	128.38 million	26.74 million
London	897,243	2.98 billion	308.12 million	2.488 billion	150.40 million	40.98 million
North East	326,257	887.62 million	124.98 million	684.51 million	66.98 million	11.14 million
North West	838,793	2.15 billion	322.63 million	1.60 billion	176.83 million	44.38 million
South East	877,585	2.59 billion	411.44 million	1.97 billion	170.24 million	36.47 million
South West	633,500	1.66 billion	277.01 million	1.23 billion	123.97 million	30.72 million
West Midlands	651,289	1.68 billion	242.16 million	1.27 billion	130.30 million	38.46 million
Yorkshire and the Humber	680,118	1.74 billion	243.24 million	1.34 billion	125.01 million	28.03 million

However, many of smokers' care needs are met informally by friends and family. It's estimated that to provide paid-for care to meet needs would cost society a further £14 billion[4]; this is not included in the overall £17 billion figure but illustrates the wider burden of smoking beyond pounds and pence.

Smoking-related fires are the leading cause of fire-related deaths, and the costs of property damage, injuries and deaths amount to another £280 million.

These figures represent profound losses to individuals and their families with smokers paying the price of addictions established in childhood throughout their lives.

Smokers also lose a large part of their income to tobacco, an estimated £12 billion in England each year, or approximately £2,000 per smoker. While the tobacco industry argue that what smokers pay in tax compensates for the cost to society, the excise tax paid for 2020/21 totalled just under £10 billion[5] in England, higher than in previous years but still nowhere near the £17.04 billion it cost society in 2019.

Other economic analysis commissioned by ASH last year found that if the country could stub out smoking for good the economic benefits would go even wider as smokers switch their spending from tobacco to other goods and services which benefit the economy more. In total this would generate around half a million jobs, with a net benefit to public finances of £600 million[6].

Deborah Arnott, Chief Executive of Action on Smoking and Health says:

'Smoking is a drain on society. It's a cost to individuals in terms of their health and wealth and a cost to us all because it undermines the productivity of our economy and places additional burdens on our NHS and care services.

The Government have delayed the tobacco control plan it promised last year which is now urgently needed with only 8 years left to achieve the goal of England being smokefree by 2030.'

Ted Aldridge, 39 from Cheshire, quit smoking last year and wants to encourage others to follow his lead:

'I had to have my ulcerated large bowel removed in 2018 as a result of colitis brought on by years of smoking and it meant that for three years I had a bag attached. I only quit smoking a year ago after I was told I could have reattachment surgery because I wanted to have clean insides in preparation for the operation. In a year staying quit I saved £2,000 in a sealed jar, enough to pay for a holiday, a widescreen TV and a new video game console. I'm passionate about persuading others to quit too – what I say is, if you hate your lungs lads, at least love your wallet?!'

14 January 2022

References

[1] Ready Reckoner tool
[2] ASH Ready Reckoner 2019 edition
[3] Reed H. The impact of smoking history on employment prospects, earnings and productivity: an analysis using UK panel data. September 2020
[4] ASH. The cost of smoking to the social care system, 2021. March 2021
[5] HMRC. National statistics: Tobacco Bulletin. November 2021
[6] ASH. Ending smoking in the UK would increase the number of UK jobs by nearly half a million. October 2021 https://ash.org.uk/media-and-news/press-releases-media-and- news/ending-smoking-in-the-uk-would-increase-the-number-of-uk-jobs-by-nearly-half- a-million/

The above information is reprinted with kind permission from *ASH*.
© 2022 Action on Smoking and Health

www.ash.org.uk

A third of smoking households in England are living in poverty with rates highest in the North

New analysis of national data commissioned by charity Action on Smoking and Health (ASH) finds that the proportion of smokers living in poverty is highest in the North and Midlands.

The new breakdown[1] published today (Wednesday 9th February) shows that In England as a whole 31% of households containing smokers live in poverty once spend on smoking is taken into account. Rates are highest in the North East where 42% of households containing smokers live in poverty, while London is lowest at 17%, but this still equates to over 80,000 households in the capital.

The link between smoking and disadvantage is well established, but this new analysis highlights how the impact of smoking on local communities is compounded in regions where household incomes are also lower. The average gross disposable household income per head in the North East is only £17,096, while in London it is £30,256.[2]

Households where people smoke are poorer because of an addiction which usually started in childhood. Two thirds of adult smokers started before they reached 18,[3] and most of them go on to become regular adult smokers.[4] Smoking is highly addictive and on average it takes thirty attempts before a smoker successfully stops for good.[5] People living with social and economic hardship tend to be more addicted, and find it harder to quit, although they try just as often.[6]

The findings also showed:

♦ The average smoker is spending just under £2,000 a year on tobacco costing England smokers a total of £12 billion.[7]

♦ When net income and smoking expenditure is taken into account, 1.16 million or 31% of households with a smoker fall below the poverty line. The residents of these houses include around 2.2 million adults below pension age, around 400,000 pension age adults and around 1 million dependent children.[8]

♦ Smokers' employment chances and average earnings are also damaged by smoking creating further hardship for people, especially those who have to give up working due to smoking-related ill health. In England 252,138 people are economically inactive due to smoking and smokers earn 8% less than non-smokers.[9]

♦ Current smokers are 5 times more likely to require social care support at home and need care on average 10 years earlier than non-smokers[10], accounting for 8% of local authority spending on adult social care.

Region	Rate of poverty among smoking households	Number of smoking households in poverty
England	31%	1,160,000
North East	42%	112,000
North West	38%	208,000
West Midlands	38%	146,000
Yorkshire and The Humber	35%	148,000
East Midlands	32%	115,000
South West	30%	110,000
South East	26%	133,000
East of England	26%	103,000
London	17%	82,000

Public Health Minister Maggie Throup said:

'Smoking has a disproportionate impact on poorer communities across the country and we're absolutely determined to hit our ambition for England to be smoke free by 2030.

'We have launched an independent review of our smoking policy, led by Javed Khan, and will publish a new plan later this year setting out how we will tackle health inequalities and level up the country.'

Deborah Arnott, Chief Executive of Action on Smoking and Health, said:

'Smoking is the single largest driver of health inequalities in England and it is shocking that it's contributing to more than two million adults living in poverty, concentrated in the most disadvantaged regions in the country.

'Behind every statistic is a human being. A real person, threatened by the debilitating health effects of smoking, and significantly poorer because of an addiction that started in childhood.

'We look forward to the forthcoming Tobacco Control Plan to achieve the Government's smokefree 2030 ambition. This will play a key role in delivering the 2030 targets to narrow the gap in life expectancy, wellbeing and productivity between the top performing and other areas set out in the Levelling Up White Paper.'

9 February 2022

References

[1] ASH, Economic and Inequalities Dashboard, 2022 https://ash.org.uk/wp-content/uploads/2022/02/Up-in-smoke_how-tobacco-drives-economic-and-health- inequalities-dashboard.zip

[2] ONS. Regional gross disposable household income, UK: 1997 to 2019. 14 October 2021

[3] Smoking (General Lifestyle Survey Overview – a report on the 2011 General Lifestyle Survey) Table 1.13

[4] Birge M, Duffy S, Miler JA, Hajek P. What proportion of people who try one cigarette become daily smokers? A meta-analysis of representative surveys. Nicotine and Tobacco Research. 2018 Nov 15;20(12):1427-33

[5] Chaiton M, Diemert L, Cohen JE, et al. Estimating the number of quit attempts it takes to quit smoking successfully in a longitudinal cohort of smokers. BMJ Open 2016;6:e011045. doi: 10.1136/bmjopen-2016-011045

[6] Loren Kock, PhD, Jamie Brown, PhD, Lion Shahab, PhD, Harry Tattan-Birch, MSc, Graham Moore, PhD, Sharon Cox, PhD, Inequalities in Smoking and Quitting-Related Outcomes Among Adults With and Without Children in the Household 2013–2019: A Population Survey in England, Nicotine & Tobacco Research, 2021

ntab211, https://doi.org/10.1093/ntr/ntab211

[7] ASH Ready Reckoner 2022: Cost of Smoking. Available at: https://ash.org.uk/ash- local-toolkit/ash-ready-reckoner-2022/

[8] H Reed (2021), Estimates of poverty in the UK adjusted for expenditure on tobacco – 2021 update. Available at: https://ash.org.uk/information-and-resources/reports- submissions/reports/smoking-and-poverty/

[9] H Reed (2020), The impact of smoking history on employment prospects, earnings and productivity: an analysis using UK panel data. Available at: https://ash.org.uk/information-and-resources/reports- submissions/reports/smokingemployability/

[10] H Reed (2021), The costs of smoking to the social care system and related costs for older people in England: 2021 revision. Available at: https://ash.org.uk/category/information-and-resources/reports-submissions/reports/

The above information is reprinted with kind permission from *ASH*.
© 2022 Action on Smoking and Health

www.ash.org.uk

Lockdown reverses 40-year decline in smoking

The biggest rise in smoking has been among 18- to 24-year-olds, who have been among the hardest hit by the pandemic.

By Charles Hymas, Home Affairs Editor

A surge in smoking among young people during the pandemic has put a 40-year decline in the habit into reverse, a study by a former Government health adviser has found.

The report projected 600,000 more smokers than previously envisaged next year as more people have taken up smoking to cope with the stress of unemployment and mental ill health during the pandemic.

This means that it will be 'virtually impossible' for the Government to meet one of its key health targets of reducing smoking to five per cent of the population by 2030 unless it takes 'drastic and immediate action' especially among young people, says the study.

The analysis by Richard Sloggett, a former policy adviser to Health Secretary Matt Hancock, shows that the proportion of smokers in the population rose from 14.8 per cent to 15 per cent in the year to March 2021 - a total of seven million people.

That is only the second increase in the past 14 years - the previous being 2014/15 - and reverses a decline that has seen the proportion of smokers fall by two-thirds from 45 per cent of the population in 1974.

The biggest rises are among 18- to 24-year-olds, who have been among the hardest hit economically and socially by the pandemic.

Some 31.8 per cent now said they had smoked at some point, up from 24.3 per cent in 2019. It was predominantly young men with one in six (16.4 per cent) describing themselves as smokers, up from 15 per cent in 2019.

Modelling by Mr Sloggett, founder of the think tank Future Health, projected that by 2030 the overall proportion of adults smoking is set to hit 7.1 per cent, well over the Government's five per cent target. This will now not be met until 2033.

'A major package of national action needs to be introduced this year including local targeted support to get back on track to eliminating smoking in England. Doing so will be fundamental to levelling-up the health inequalities that have been so clearly exposed by the pandemic,' he said.

The research also found big regional disparities. Of the highest 10 areas for smoking rates, only one area (Dartford) is classified as being in the South of England.

Corby had the highest rates at 27.5 per cent, followed by Lincoln (24.8 per cent), Blackpool (23.4 per cent), Great Yarmouth (23.4 per cent), Kingston upon Hull (22.2 per cent), North East Lincolnshire (22.2 per cent), Fenland (21.9 per cent) Burnley (21.5 per cent), Barrow-in-Furness (21.4 per cent).

By contrast, of the areas in the bottom 10 for smoking rates, only one (Ribble Valley) is classified as being in the North of England; with seven in the south of England and two in the Midlands.

Hart in Hampshire and St Albans in Hertfordshire are the only two local authorities in England which have less than five per cent of the adult population who are smokers.

Mr Sloggett said: 'Some areas of the country are currently four or five times above the stated five per cent ambition level and such local variation presents a major barrier to delivering on the target.'

17 May 2021

The above information is reprinted with kind permission from *The Telegraph*.
© Telegraph Media Group Limited 2022

www.telegraph.co.uk

Smoking-related cancer twice as prevalent among poor in England

Overall cancer rates are higher among the wealthy, finds Cancer Research UK – but smoking and its cancers are now concentrated among the poor.

By Denis Campbell

Smoking causes almost twice as many cancer cases among the poor than the well-off, according to new findings that underline the close link between cigarettes and deprivation.

About 11,247 cases of cancer caused by smoking are diagnosed among the poorest 20% of people in England each year, but far fewer – 6,200 – among those in the top 20% income bracket.

Cancer Research UK, which produced the estimates, said the findings underlined why ministers should impose a levy on tobacco firms to help fund the cost of helping tobacco addicts to quit.

'It's very concerning that smoking causes more cancer cases in more deprived groups,' said Michelle Mitchell, Cancer Research UK's chief executive.

The difference in cancer incidence between rich and poor is so great that, combined with cuts to stop-smoking services in recent years, it threatens the government's target of England becoming smoke-free by 2030, she added.

The number of people smoking would need to fall from its current record low of 15.5% to just 5% in order for that ambition to be achieved. While the proportion of people lighting up has fallen significantly over the last 20 years, it is increasingly concentrated among poorer groups.

People in the most deprived communities are two and a half times more likely to smoke than the top fifth of people by income, which is the main reason for the greater number of cancers there, CRUK said.

'This stark differential in cancer rates exists because of the iron chain linking smoking and disadvantage. Around a quarter of those who are unemployed or in routine and manual occupations smoke, compared with fewer than one in 10 working in management or the professions,' said Deborah Arnott, chief executive of the anti-smoking charity ASH.

Analysis by CRUK found that about 53,227 cancers a year are diagnosed among the poorest 20% of people in England as measured by the Office of National Statistics's index of multiple deprivation. Of those, an estimated 11,247 – 21% of the total – are caused directly by smoking, it said.

More cancer cases occur in the wealthiest 20% – an estimated 63,828. However, far fewer of them – 6,200 – are the result of someone smoking, and they represent a much smaller percentage (10%) of all cases of cancer that occur in that part of the population.

Prof Linda Bauld, a public health expert at Edinburgh university, said: 'This new study found that more cancer cases are caused by smoking in the most deprived 20% of the population. This is due to more people smoking in this group, likely because of several factors such as exposure to smoking, access to cigarettes, tobacco industry marketing, housing and income pressures, and access to health and social care, information and education.'

Arnott backed CRUK's call for tobacco companies to be forced to contribute to a smoke-free fund, based on 'the polluter pays' principle. 'Tobacco manufacturers make extreme profits off the backs of the poor. The time has come to make them pay to end the epidemic that they and they alone have caused,' she said.

2 August 2021

The above information is reprinted with kind permission from *The Guardian*.
© 2022 Guardian News and Media Limited

www.theguardian.com

Nicotine addiction & side effects on the body

By John Dicey & Paul Baker. Reviewed by: Dr Vishal U S Rao

What is nicotine?

Nicotine is a chemical compound produced naturally in the nightshade family of plants. It is an alkaloid which accumulates in the leaves of the tobacco plant and to a much lesser degree in potatoes, aubergine and tomatoes[1]. It is found in cigarettes, cigars, pipe tobacco, chewing tobacco, wet and dry snuff, E-cigarettes, most vaping juices and heat not burn devices.

How does nicotine work? What are the nicotine side effects on the body?

When tobacco smoke or vapour is inhaled, nicotine is absorbed through the mucosal linings in the nose, mouth and lungs and travels through the bloodstream to the brain. When sniffed, snussed (via pouches) or chewed it is absorbed through membranes in the mouth and nose. It then travels through the body, via the bloodstream to the brain. It is also possible to absorb it through the skin.

When smoked nicotine reaches the brain in about seven seconds[2]. It is about the same when vaped, around 8-20 seconds. Nicotine reaches the central nervous system in about 3-5 minutes when tobacco is chewed.

Neuroscience still hasn't fully understood how nicotine affects the brain or how addiction works but more is being learnt all the time.

Is there a high?

Some smokers claim that the feeling of dizziness or light-headedness after they haven't smoked for a while is like a 'high' – but when you think about it – it isn't is it? It's just dizzy and you can get exactly the same feeling by spinning around on the spot for ten seconds.

Does nicotine relieve anxiety or make you feel depressed?

Some people claim that smoking helps with depression and anxiety but if this were true then surely smokers would be less anxious and less depressed than non-smokers? Yet research shows the exact opposite – that they are much more anxious and more depressed than non-smokers. Tragically there's no doubt that a good portion of people who live with depression and anxiety are drawn into smoking by the flawed belief that nicotine might help them handle their condition – that's all part of the brainwashing.

How does nicotine affect dopamine?

Humans are programmed to seek out dopamine elevating activities to ensure good health, happiness and longevity/survival. Examples are making love, eating, listening to music, hugging children/animals/your partner/a friend, socialising, and exercising. These are natural/normal/healthy activities/behaviours that the normally functioning 'reward system' is designed to reinforce.

Back when smoking was at its peak, we didn't know how nicotine and other drugs affected the brain. Since then we have learned a great deal about a function of the brain known colloquially as reward pathways.

In the brain dopamine functions as a neurotransmitter – a chemical released by neurons (nerve cells) to send signals to other nerve cells. The reward pathways play a major role in the motivational component of reward-motivated, or reinforced behaviour. Can you imagine the disruption that can be caused to this natural, instinctive process by the introduction of a highly addictive drug, one which appears to relieve the discomfort created by the first dose, and every subsequent dose?

In 2019 one of the world's leading academics in the field of nicotine addiction, Professor Robert West stated publicly, 'Nicotine causes dopamine release by nerve cells that make up the 'reward system' in the brain, including the nucleus accumbens– a part of the brain involved in learning to do things. The dopamine release tells the brain to pay attention to the situation and what the smoker was just doing – and do the same thing next time they're in that same situation. So, a link is forged between the impulse to smoke and situations in which smoking normally happens'. Importantly, Professor West went on to add, 'Crucially, the smoker doesn't have to feel any pleasure or enjoyment for this to work.'

How does nicotine make you feel?

A smoker's first experience of nicotine is normally at worst extremely unpleasant, and at best, a little unpleasant. For the sake of understanding this, smokers have to ignore the feelings aroused by the circumstances surrounding their first cigarette; the peer pressure & praise, the feeling of rebelliousness, the feeling of fitting in, the sense of appearing stylish, sophisticated, or macho. None of those are caused by the introduction of nicotine to the body, they're all to do with the environment.

How does nicotine produce a feeling of pleasure?

So, most smokers remember the physical effect of their first cigarettes as being unpleasant and this alone disproves any notion that nicotine's initial introduction to the body and brain caused 'pleasure'. Whatever impact nicotine has on dopamine levels when first introduced to the body – it's certainly not pleasurable. In fact, most people's first cigarette is so unpleasant and unrewarding it convinces them that they could never become addicted. The reason smokers develop a deep-seated belief that smoking IS pleasurable is explained by Professor West perfectly.

Nicotine withdrawal is the result of the first ever cigarette a nicotine addict smoked. It is momentarily 'relieved' by the next cigarette. The brain concludes, non-consciously, 'next time you feel nicotine withdrawal – do that again!'. In other words, the behaviour of lighting a cigarette in response to experiencing nicotine withdrawal is reinforced every time a smoker lights a cigarette regardless of the fact that the next cigarette will also cause nicotine withdrawal.

Whether a smoker is in a happy situation, a concentration situation, a sad situation, a stress situation, a relaxing situation, a boring situation, or a lonely situation they simultaneously experience nicotine withdrawal, and respond by lighting a cigarette, thereby immediately feeling better than a moment before and oblivious to the fact that that cigarette will perpetuate nicotine withdrawal once it is smoked .

It's no wonder they think cigarettes help them to be happy or to concentrate, or to cope with sadness and stress, and to help them relax or cope with boredom or loneliness! It's got nothing to do with genuine pleasure or genuine improvement of mood. And every single time they light a cigarette in one of those situations – the brain concludes, non- consciously, 'next time that happens – do that again!'.

Non-smokers don't have to deal with any of the mental and physical aggravation of being addicted to nicotine. They don't suffer nicotine poisoning, nicotine withdrawal or the aberrational/unnatural impact nicotine has on dopamine and their behaviour.

Smoking damages your heart and your blood circulation, increasing the risk of conditions such as coronary heart disease, heart attack, stroke, peripheral vascular disease (damaged blood vessels) and cerebrovascular disease (damaged arteries that supply blood to your brain).

Once in the brain it mimics acetycholine a natural neurotransmitter which naturally occurs in the brain activating particular types of acetycholine receptors.

Acetycholine is known to help maintain healthy respiration, heart function, muscle movement and cognitive function such as memory.

Nicotine increases adrenaline which in turn increases blood pressure, respiration, and heart rate[4].

Is nicotine an addictive drug?

A drug is defined as a medicine or a substance which has a psychological effect after being ingested or otherwise introduced into the body.

How addictive are cigarettes?

Nicotine is a highly addictive drug. You can suffer from cigarette addiction otherwise known as smoking addiction, or you can suffer from vaping addiction. Of course any product that contains nicotine will be addictive, including nicotine patches and gum, inhalators, lozenges, mouth sprays, nose sprays, chewing tobacco (or dip), and snus (otherwise known as nicotine pouches).

Addiction is the term commonly applied to maladaptive drug seeking behaviour, often taken despite knowledge of negative health consequences[5]. The World Health Organisation (WHO) states that nicotine meets the established criteria for a drug that produces addiction, specifically, dependence and withdrawal.

Nicotine dependence is an anomaly. Although the phrase is commonly used by doctors and academics it is a statement of fact that no-one is dependent on nicotine. No-one needs nicotine in order to function properly. The fact is that nicotine makes addicts FEEL dependent on it. This is a very different state of affairs to BEING dependent on it.

Why are nicotine and cigarettes addictive?

As explained above nicotine changes how the brain functions. Whether one has a smoking addiction, in the form of cigarette addiction, or one vapes, chews, or snusses, regular intake of nicotine changes the number

of cholinergic receptors and their sensitivity. This leads to nicotine tolerance.

In fact Nicotine addiction, often described as nicotine dependence, is at least as addictive as heroin and cocaine per the US Surgeon General[6].

How much nicotine and cigarettes does it take to get addicted?

It takes just one puff of one cigarette, cigar, pipe, vape, or joint with tobacco in, to cause someone to become addicted[8]. The same goes for snus and chewing tobacco.

There have been many studies conducted looking at all the different parameters such as gender, social structure, socioeconomic variables, parental and peer smoking, academic achievement, ethnicity, mental health, and many others to see how these affected chances of nicotine addiction. Research now postulates that the progression is essentially universal[7].

How long does nicotine take to leave the body?

The Centre for Disease Control and Prevention (CDC) says that around 2 hours after ingesting nicotine the body will have removed half of it. It will take several weeks to become very low.

Nicotine side effects: short and long term

What does nicotine do to your body?

Nicotine is the fundamental cause of addiction among tobacco users. Nicotine adversely affects many organs as shown in human and animal studies. Its biological effects are widespread and extend to all systems of the body including cardiovascular, respiratory, renal and reproductive systems. Nicotine has also been found to be carcinogenic in several studies. It promotes tumorigenesis by affecting cell proliferation, angiogenesis and apoptotic pathways. It causes resistance to the chemotherapeutic agents. Any substantive beneficial effect of nicotine on human body is yet to be proven.[9]

Is nicotine bad for you?

Undoubtedly, nicotine is bad for you. It doesn't occur naturally in our diet (other than tiny traces in aubergine, tomatoes, potatoes, and green peppers). Nicotine is poisonous and can easily kill when consumed in large doses. As little as 1 teaspoon of liquid nicotine, as used in vape juice, can be fatal for the average 26-pound toddler.[10]

Negative effects of nicotine

Aside from health issues – being addicted to nicotine in any form isn't fun. It controls what the addict does, when they do it, and how they feel when they're doing it. The impact of nicotine addiction, and repeated failed attempts to break it, causes issues with self-esteem, self-respect, as well as relationships. This is all quite aside from the costs involved.

Dangers of nicotine

There are the health risks, the cost, the slavery of being addicted, the risk of overdose, as well as the impact on the body of whatever carrier is used to deliver the nicotine (cigarettes, vape, chewing tobacco etc).

Nicotine health risks

Nicotine is highly addictive as shown above and has many side-effects not least the desire to smoke cigarettes, chew tobacco or vape.

Nicotine side effects [11-17]

Blood circulation

Taking nicotine results in blood vessels constricting and narrowing, limiting the blood that flows to your organs as well as thickening of the blood.

Short term

- Increased tendency to clot
- Increased blood pressure and heart rate

Long term

- Atherosclerosis (plaque forms on the artery wall)
- Increase in size of aorta

How does nicotine affect the brain?

Taking nicotine affects the efficiency of the limbic and paralimbic areas of the brain. These regions are responsible for attention, memory and learning.

Short term

- Dizziness
- Poor sleeping

Long term

- Bad dreams and nightmares
- Headaches

Heart

Taking nicotine results in blood vessels constricting and narrowing, limiting the blood that flows to the heart.

Short term

- Chest pain
- Uneven heartbeats

Long term

- Increased risk of stroke
- Constriction of the coronary artery

Gastrointestinal system

Nicotine interacts with all parts of the digestive system leading to many harmful effects.

Short term

- Hiccups or belching
- Dry mouth
- Nausea

Long term

- Diarrhea
- Constipation
- Heartburn
- Ulceration

Reproductive system

Nicotine damages all parts of the reproductive system in both men and women including the genetic material of sperm cells.

Short term

- Sperm and semen quality suffer
- Egg cells damage
- Affects the menstrual cycle making it more irregular

Long term

- Decrease the sperm count
- Reduction in the volume of sperm
- Changes to cervical mucus (affects how sperm reaches the egg)
- Problems with fallopian tubes
- Infertility in both men and women

Other

Taking nicotine has harmful effects on other parts of the body not least the respiratory system.

Short term

- Throat or mouth soreness
- Watery eyes or mouth
- Coughing
- Sneezing
- Suppression of the immune system

Long term

- Changes in taste
- Wheezing
- Narrowing of the lung airways
- Development of emphysema
- Pancreatic cancer
- Breast cancer
- Increased risk of developing cataracts
- Increased risk of chronic kidney disease

7 January 2022

References

1. Harm reduction in nicotine addiction: helping people who can't quit. A report by The Tobacco Advisory Group at the Royal College of Physicians London, Royal College of Physicians, 2007
2. Chen Li-Lun FDA summary of adverse reports on electronic cigarettes (2013) 15(2): 615-616 Nicotine Tob Res 2013:15;615-6
4. Hoffman D, Hoffman I The changing cigarette,1950-1955 J Toxic Environ Health 1997;50(4):306-364
5. World Health Organisation Report on gender, women and the tobacco epidemic
6. Preventing tobacco use among young people: reporting certain general. Centres for disease control and prevention, National Centre for chronic disease prevention health promotion 1994 & US Department of health and human services. The health consequences of smoking: nicotine addiction: report to the Surgeon General 1988
7. DiFranza, Rigotti, McNeill initial symptoms of nicotine dependence in adolescence. Tobacco control.2000;9:413-318
8. Scragg, Wellman diminished autonomy over tobacco can appear with the first cigarettes. Addictive behaviours.2008;33:689-698
9. A Mishra, P Chaturvedi, S Datta, S Sinukumar Harmful effects of nicotine Indian J Med Paediatr Oncol. 2015 Jan-Mar; 36(1): 24–31
10. Nicotine Poisoning: Can You Overdose? WebMD
11. The hazardous effects of tobacco smoking on male fertility Jing-Bo Dai, Zhao-Xia Wang, and Zhong-Dong Qiao Asian J Androl. 2015 Nov-Dec; 17(6): 954–960
12. How Tobacco Smoke Causes Disease: The Biology and Behavioral Basis for Smoking-Attributable Disease: A Report of the Surgeon General Centers for Disease Control and Prevention (US); National Center for Chronic Disease Prevention and Health Promotion (US); Office on Smoking and Health (US). Atlanta (GA): Centers for Disease Control and Prevention (US); 2010
13. Harmful effects of nicotine Aseem Mishra, Pankaj Chaturvedi, Indian J Med Paediatr Oncol. 2015 Jan-Mar; 36(1): 24–31
14. Smoking and the Digestive System National Institute of Diabetes and Digestive and Kidney diseases
15. Smoking and Respiratory Diseases John Hopkins
16. Health Effects of Cigarette Smoking Centre for Disease Control and Prevention
17. What are the health risks of smoking? NHS

The above information is reprinted with kind permission from Allen Carr's Easyway.
© 2022 Allen Carr's Easyway (International) Ltd

www.allencarr.com

Silent sleep danger for smokers uncovered in world-first study

We all know smoking is bad for you but scientists have now discovered people who have sleep apnoea - known as the silent killer - are putting themselves in even greater danger of future health complications.

In a first study of its kind, scientists from the Heart Research Institute (HRI) have made the link between amounts of nicotine in the blood and the amount of time people have less oxygen while they're sleeping.

Sleep apnoea occurs when a person's throat and upper airway become partly or completely blocked during sleep, causing short periods where breathing stops.

In a new paper published in ESC Heart Failure, HRI scientists found increases in nicotine levels were associated with a 2.3 minute increase in the time spent with oxygen saturations below 90 per cent.

One of the markers of severity of sleep apnoea is time spent with an oxygen saturation less than 90 per cent.

Lead researcher Dr John O'Sullivan, of HRI's Cardiometabolic Disease Group, said this meant that for every cigarette a person smoked, they were more likely to have 'dangerously low' levels of oxygen.

'People who spend more time with an oxygen saturation less than 90 per cent end up with more cardiovascular death than people who don't,' Dr O'Sullivan said.

'We know smoking is bad for the heart – it's one of the major risks for heart attacks – and although smoking is known to reduce oxygen concentration in the blood, the interaction of smoking with sleep apnoea has not been quantified. Using blood concentrations of the major nicotine metabolite, we were able for the first time to quantify the effect of smoking on oxygen concentrations at night in people with sleep apnoea.

'A standardised increase in levels of this metabolite was associated with 2.3 more minutes with an oxygen concentration less than 90 per cent in people with sleep apnoea. Time with an oxygen concentration less than 90 per cent is a proven indicator of bad cardiovascular outcome.'

Scientists know sleep apnoea and congestive heart failure commonly co-exist but with their interaction unclear, Dr O'Sullivan's team used hundreds of small molecules called metabolites to understand this interaction.

'Believe it or not, stiff heart failure – when the heart muscle can still pump blood but is stiff and cannot relax properly – is the most common form of heart failure today and we have almost no treatment options,' Dr O'Sullivan said.

'We measured molecules in the blood called metabolites and looked at the changes in these metabolites and related these to the severity of sleep apnoea.'

Metabolomics is a relatively new field of study that investigates metabolites, which are the components of your metabolism and play key roles in disease. They can provide insight into how one disease is linked to another, like in this case the consequences of sleep apnoea and heart failure. Several metabolites are also key fuels for the working heart, and others form the units of energy by which the heart works.

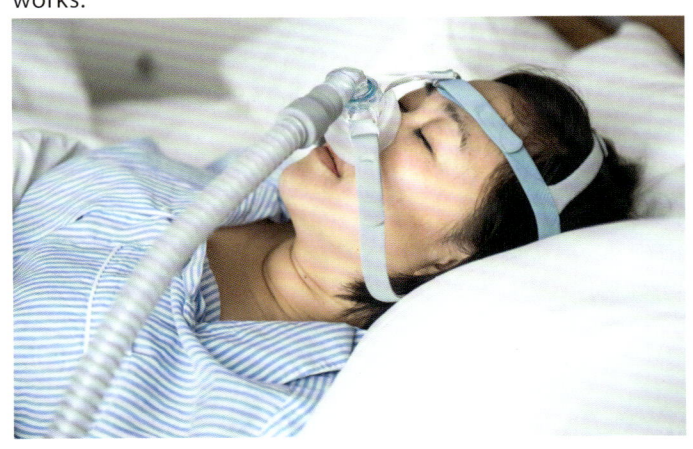

The team studied metabolites and lipids in 1,919 people from the Framingham Heart Study and 1,524 participants of the Women's Health Initiative, both US studies.

Dr O'Sullivan said Framingham was known as the 'town that changed America' because of the multi-generational study that started in 1948 that subsequently identified the cardiovascular risk factors we still use today. Much research using this study is openly available internationally, enabling researchers around the world.

'Accurate measurement of disease combined with blood metabolite levels is far more accurate than self-reported questionnaires – that's one of the strengths of this study,' he said.

Although sleep apnoea is very common (up to one in four adults), its consequences and interactions with other diseases remain poorly understood. There are almost no studies with sleep study data, heart failure data, and metabolomic data in the same individuals – this is a major novelty of this study.

Other findings in this study include new insights into the relationship between lipid storage, energy storage, and heart size and structure.

Dr Melissa Farnham, who was involved in the study, is the leader of the Cardiovascular Neuroscience Group at HRI, and her research focuses on how the brain responds to sleep apnoea.

11 November 2021

The above information is reprinted with kind permission from The Heart Research Institute (UK) © 2022 HRI. All Rights Reserved.

www.hriuk.org

Second-hand smoke: when you work in others' homes, where do their rights end and yours begin?

An article from The Conversation.

By Ruaraidh Dobson, Research Fellow Institute for Social Marketing, University of Stirling & Sean Semple, Associate Professor Institute for Social Marketing, University of Stirling

Imagine someone walking into a cafe, sitting down at a table and lighting up a cigarette. In the UK – and other countries where smoking in indoor public places is banned – that would be almost unthinkable. In the 15 years since smoking bans came into effect across Britain, smoking inside has gone from a fact of life to an aberration, and the nation's health is all the better for it.

Strokes, heart problems and asthma attacks have all fallen since the bans were introduced, particularly among people who used to spend their working lives in smoky environments. However, smoking isn't banned in all workplaces and lots of workers still breathe in smoke when they're doing their jobs, such as tradespeople, care workers and meter readers.

In our recent study, we estimated that around one million UK workers are regularly exposed to second-hand smoke while they work. Of those, the most severely affected included home care workers – nurses, carers and other professionals who provide help at home for those who need it most. In the course of our research, we've seen these workers exposed to levels of smoke higher than those you'd find during smog in highly polluted cities like Delhi.

Those high levels of second-hand smoke could be a real problem. Even short periods of exposure to high levels of small particulates (like those in second-hand smoke) have been linked to heart attacks and other circulatory problems in vulnerable people, as well as asthma attacks. Over the longer term, regular exposure to smoke could increase the risk of heart disease, lung problems and even stroke.

This seems like a poor reward for someone who spends their life caring for others. That's particularly true when we consider that care workers are often badly paid, coming from sections of society that already suffer health inequalities and experience shorter lifespans.

Policies to protect

Many care organisations, including the NHS, have policies designed to address these problems. Often this involves asking clients not to smoke for an hour before a care worker attends their home.

However, we know from our previous research that second-hand smoke can remain in a home at harmful levels for more than five hours after a cigarette is smoked – one hour isn't enough to clear the air. And even if it were, our research suggests that this guidance isn't being followed, with smokers lighting up even when workers are in their homes.

There are serious concerns about the health of these workers. But there is a tension at the heart of this problem: when your workplace is someone else's home, whose rights come first? Smokers may choose to smoke at home, particularly those with existing health and mobility issues (who are more likely to receive care) where getting outside is difficult.

It's not good for their health (and certainly not for anyone else who lives with them) but it's their choice and their right. That said, if your job requires you to enter an environment and accept any health risks that come with it, don't you deserve clean air like any other worker?

There's no clear, universally acceptable way to balance these two positions. But we need to think clearly about risks and rights to find a way forward between these two competing ideas: the right to choose what you do in your own home versus the right of everyone to clean air at work.

The pandemic may have changed which solutions people find acceptable. For instance, people are now fairly comfortable wearing masks indoors. It's possible that wearing high-quality N95 masks could reduce the number of smoke particles that workers breathe in to a level that leads to fewer health problems.

But this is difficult to do. Many of the thousands of chemicals in second-hand smoke can't be filtered out as they're gases rather than solid particles, so the World Health Organisation says that there's no such thing as a safe level of tobacco smoke. Still, for short visits, this might bring the risk down to a more acceptable level.

Other COVID-related changes might include a better understanding of the effect of ventilation. As it's become better understood that the virus is airborne, improving building ventilation has risen up the agenda. That can be difficult in older houses, but some studies have shown success using air cleaners to combat small particles in homes – but these devices face some of the same problems as masks and do little to remove the harmful gases produced by smoking.

Calling time on smoking

If this doesn't work, we might need a more drastic solution. Given the serious health effects of second-hand smoke exposure and the estimated 800,000 premature deaths it causes globally each year, society might choose to reject the idea of a 'right to smoke in the home' entirely.

After all, smoking isn't essential even for smokers, with nicotine replacement products and e-cigarettes widely (and cheaply) available, and smokers in the UK are already required to keep private cars smoke-free when children are travelling. How we view smoking in the presence of children is changing. In the future, we might see smoking in the home as unacceptable, given the toxic chemicals it releases into the air.

Smoke-free policies not only benefit those exposed to second-hand smoke – often they lead to smokers kicking the habit. Could all homes go smoke-free one day? That wouldn't just benefit care workers, but also the one in nine Scottish children currently living in smoky homes. It's difficult to imagine – but so were smoke-free pubs less than two decades ago.

17 June 2021

The above information is reprinted with kind permission from The Conversation © 2010-2022, The Conversation Trust (UK) Limited

www.theconversation.com

E-cigarettes & Vaping

Chapter 2

8 things to know about e-cigarettes

Vaping is not risk free but is far less harmful than smoking. Our advice remains that people who smoke are better to switch completely to vaping but if you have never been a smoker, don't start to vape.

This blog, published to coincide with PHE's latest independent evidence report, looks at some of the most common misconceptions around e-cigarettes and provides the facts.

1. E-cigarettes and the US lung injury outbreak

Last August, vapers began to arrive at emergency rooms across the US suffering from serious lung injuries. It was not immediately clear what was behind the outbreak, which led to 68 deaths over the following months. Based partly on the fact that the outbreak affected a very specific population and how the rate of new cases peaked and fell we wrote to the Lancet to explain that a 'bad batch' of illicit cannabis vaping products may be to blame. However, in response to the outbreak, regulators around the world started taking nicotine vaping products off the market whilst tobacco cigarettes remained available, discouraging smokers from switching.

US authorities have since identified vitamin E acetate added to cannabis products as a 'primary cause' of the outbreak. Vitamin E acetate is banned from UK regulated nicotine-containing e-cigarettes.

2. Vaping and heart disease

A controversial study that reported that vapers had the same risk of heart disease as smokers was recently withdrawn by the journal as it did not take into consideration that almost all the vapers involved were current or former smokers.

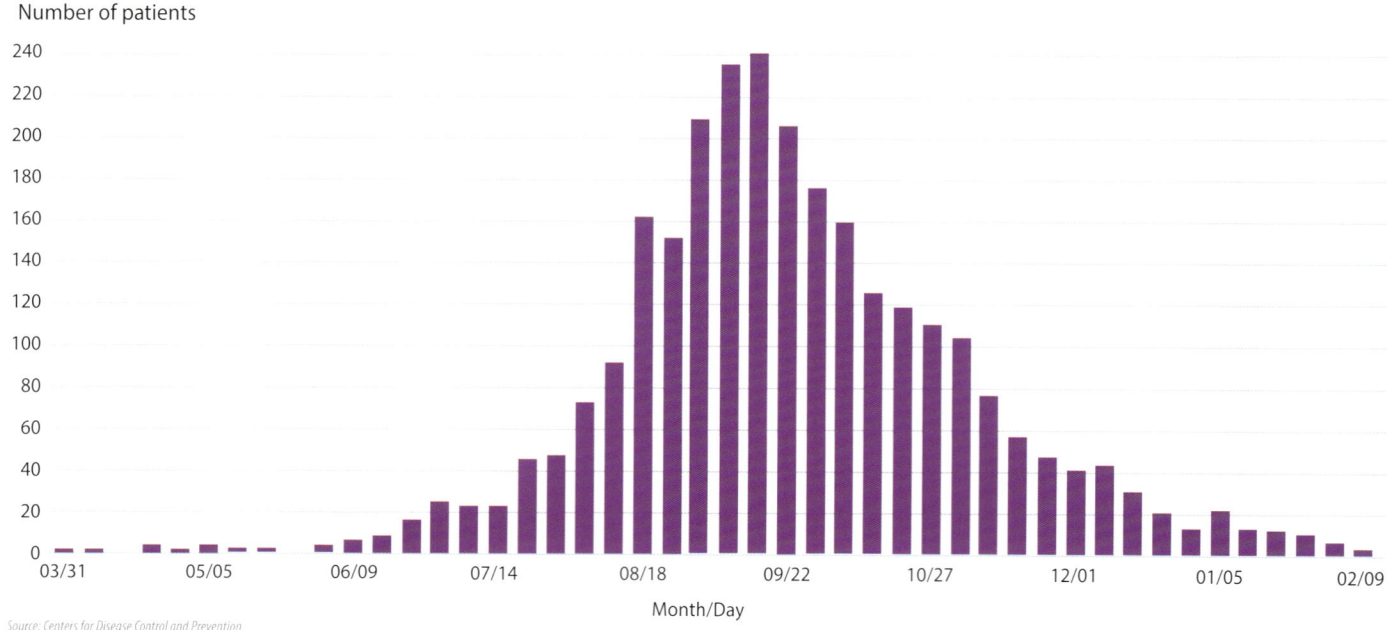

Dates of symptom onset and hospital admission for patients with lung injury associated with e-cigarette use, or vaping – United States, March 31, 2019-February 15, 2020

Source: Centers for Disease Control and Prevention

A better understanding of the effect of e-cigarettes on the heart is beginning to emerge. A randomised control trial that measured the vascular effects of smokers switching to vaping was published in December with encouraging results. Those who switched to e-cigarettes completely experienced the largest improvement in their vascular health, getting close to the healthy 'control'. Larger studies with longer follow up will provide greater confidence.

3. Harms compared to smoking

Only one in three adults in England knows that vaping is far less harmful than smoking. Yet in 2018 the US National Academies of Sciences, Engineering and Medicine (NASEM) found that the available evidence suggests e-cigarettes are 'far less harmful' than conventional smoking.

Public Health England's 2015 independent evidence report, concluded that: 'While vaping may not be 100% safe, most of the chemicals causing smoking-related disease are absent and the chemicals which are present pose limited danger.'

More research is needed into the relative harms of e-cigarettes. Last month PHE commissioned the final and most ambitious report in the current series of e-cigarette updates. A team that combines authors of PHE's previous reports with other international experts are starting work on a wide range of systematic reviews, including one on safety, to permit our most authoritative assessment in 2022.

4. Harms of nicotine

Four out of 10 smokers and ex-smokers wrongly think nicotine causes most of the smoking-related cancers, when evidence shows nicotine actually carries minimal risk of harm to health. Although nicotine is the reason people become addicted to smoking, it is the thousands of other chemicals contained in cigarette smoke that cause almost all of the harm.

5. Quitting smoking

A major UK NIHR funded clinical trial was published in February 2019. Involving nearly 900 participants, it found that in Local Stop Smoking Services, a standard e-cigarette was twice as effective at helping smokers to quit compared with the quitters' choice of combination nicotine replacement therapy (NRT).

A separate study from UCL found that e-cigarettes helped an additional 50-70,000 smokers in England to quit in a single year.

6. Harms to bystanders

The evidence is clear that exposure to second hand smoke is harmful, which is why the UK has laws prohibiting smoking in enclosed public places and workplaces. These laws do not cover vaping and organisations are free to make their own policies on vaping on their premises.

E-cigarette liquid is typically composed of nicotine, propylene glycol and/or glycerine, and flavourings. Unlike cigarettes, there is no side-stream vapour emitted by an e-cigarette into the atmosphere, just the exhaled aerosol.

Our 2018 report found there have been no identified health risks of passive vaping to bystanders and our 2022 report will review the evidence again. People with asthma and other respiratory conditions can be sensitive to a range of environmental irritants, and PHE advises organisations to take this into account and make adjustments to policies where appropriate.

7. Vaping and youth smoking

Our latest report found no evidence to support concern that e-cigarettes are increasing youth smoking. UK surveys show that young people are experimenting with e-cigarettes, but regular use is rare and confined almost entirely to those who already smoke. Meanwhile, smoking rates among young people in the UK continue to decline.

Concerns that e-cigarettes might be 'renormalising smoking' were addressed in a 2019 study. PHE continues to monitor the trends in vaping and smoking among young people. We have recently commissioned research on the role of flavourings in youth vaping and in adult switching.

8. E-cigarettes regulation

The UK has well established regulation for e-cigarettes. Under the Tobacco and Related Products Regulations 2016, nicotine containing e-cigarette products are subject to minimum standards of quality and safety, as well as packaging and labelling requirements to provide consumers with the information they need to make informed choices.

Advertising is tightly restricted and all products must be notified by manufacturers with detailed information to the UK Medicines and Healthcare products Regulatory Agency, which prohibits certain ingredients.

This autumn an international report ranked the UK top for action to block tobacco industry influence. PHE regularly advises local authorities to reject approaches from tobacco companies.

5 March 2020

The above information is reprinted with kind permission from UK Health Security Agency.
© Crown copyright 2022
This information is licensed under the Open Government Licence v3.0
To view this licence, visit http://www.nationalarchives.gov.uk/doc/open-government-licence/

www.ukhsa.blog.gov.uk

Vaping better than nicotine replacement therapy for stopping smoking, evidence suggests

As number of vapers in England plateaus, incorrect perceptions of its relative risks compared to smoking may be discouraging smokers from using vaping to quit.

By Public Health England

Public Health England's (PHE) seventh independent report on vaping in England, carried out by researchers at King's College London, found that:

- nicotine vaping products were the most popular aid (27.2%) used by smokers trying to quit in England in 2020
- it is estimated that in 2017, more than 50,000 smokers stopped smoking with the aid of a vaping product who would otherwise have carried on smoking
- 38% of smokers in 2020 believed that vaping is as harmful as smoking – 15% believed that vaping is more harmful
- using a vaping product as part of a quit attempt in local stop smoking services had some of the highest quit success rates – between 59.7% and 74% in 2019 and 2020

The report takes an in-depth look at the latest evidence on the effectiveness of nicotine vaping products in helping people to stop smoking. The report also provides an update on the use of nicotine vaping products among young people and adults and examines the data on people's perception of risk.

Coronavirus (COVID-19) is likely to have had an impact on smoking and vaping behaviours in both adults and young people. However, it is still too early to assess the full effect of the pandemic, with much of the data examined in this report being pre-pandemic.

In England in 2020, nicotine vaping products were the most popular aid used by smokers trying to quit, with 27.2% of smokers using a vaping product compared with 18.2% using nicotine replacement therapy (NRT) products (such as patches and gum) and 4.4% using the prescription medicine varenicline.

Evidence over the years suggests that as the use of vaping products in quit attempts increases, the number of successful quits in England also increases. It is estimated that in 2017, more than 50,000 smokers stopped smoking with the aid of a vaping product who would otherwise have carried on smoking. Data from systematic reviews since PHE's 2018 report show that vaping products were significantly more effective for helping people stop smoking than NRT.

Those using a vaping product as part of their quit attempt in local, stop smoking services have some of the highest quit-success rates – between 59.7% and 74% in 2019 to 2020.

Vaping has plateaued in adults and young people since the last PHE report in March 2020.

Around 4.8% of young people (aged 11 to 18 years) reported vaping at least once a month – the same as last year – and most of these were either current or former smokers (only 0.8% of young people who had never smoked currently vape). Smoking prevalence among young people, including

those who smoked sometimes or more than once a week, was 6.7% in March 2020, similar to March 2019, at 6.3%. The law bans the sale of smoking and vaping products to under 18s but age-of-sale violations are being reported.

Similar to last year, around 6% of adults are current vapers, equating to about 2.7 million adult vapers in England. Smoking prevalence continues to fall and is between 13.8% and 16% depending on the survey. Vaping prevalence was between 17.5% and 20.1% among current smokers, around 11% among former smokers and between 0.3% and 0.6% among those who have never smoked. The proportion of vapers who also smoke, or 'dual users', has declined since 2012.

There are still concerns around increasing misperception of the relative risk caused by vaping products, compared to smoked tobacco. In 2020, 38% of smokers believed that vaping is as harmful as smoking and 15% believed that vaping is more harmful. This is out of line with expert reviews from the UK and US (United States), concluding that using regulated nicotine vaping products is far less harmful than smoking.

Professor John Newton, Director of Health Improvement at PHE said:

'Smoking is still the leading preventable cause of premature death and disease – killing almost 75,000 people in England in 2019. The best thing that a smoker can do is to stop smoking completely and the evidence shows that vaping is one of the most effective quit aids available, helping around 50,000 smokers quit a year.

Thousands more could have quit except for unfounded safety fears about e-cigarettes. The evidence has been clear for some time that, while not risk-free vaping is far less harmful than smoking.

For anyone who smokes, particularly those who have already tried other methods, we strongly recommend they try vaping and stop smoking – ideally with additional support from their local stop smoking service for the very best chance of quitting for good.'

PHE's advice remains that smokers should switch to vaping products to help them quit smoking, but non-smokers should not take up vaping. Vaping products contain significantly less harmful chemicals than cigarettes but are not without some risks.

PHE has commissioned a full review of the evidence on the safety of vaping products, which will be published next year in 2022. King's College London is working with a number of different researchers from the UK and US (United States) (including some who contributed to the National Academies of Sciences, Engineering and Medicine's e-cigarette report in in 2018) to conduct this review.

Professor Ann McNeill, Professor of Tobacco Addiction at King's College London, and lead author of the report, said:

Our report draws together findings from randomised controlled trials, stop smoking services and population studies and concludes that nicotine vaping products are an effective way of successfully quitting smoking.

What is concerning is that smokers, particularly those from disadvantaged groups, incorrectly and increasingly believe that vaping is as harmful as smoking. This is not true and means fewer smokers try vaping.

The goal for 2030 is to be smokefree in England. The development of a new Tobacco Control Plan and this year's review of the Tobacco and Related Products Regulations 2016 is an opportunity to ensure that the regulations around vaping are appropriate. The regulations are also hoped to help smokers to quit, while not attracting people who have never smoked.

Deborah Arnott, Chief Executive of ASH, said,

Rightly, since e-cigarettes emerged as an alternative to smoking, the government has sought to strike a balance between helping smokers to quit and protecting children. As ASH research included in the report for PHE shows, e-cigarette use among 11 to 18 year olds has to date remained low, but on the downside their potential as an adult quitting aid has not been fully realised.

As we strive to achieve a smokefree nation by 2030 more needs to be done to support adult smokers who could benefit from switching to do so, while eliminating loopholes in the laws which could be used to promote products to teenagers.

Michelle Mitchell, Cancer Research UK's Chief Executive, said:

E-cigarettes are a still relatively new product – they aren't risk-free as we don't yet know their long-term impact. We strongly discourage people who haven't smoked from using them, particularly young people. But research so far shows that vaping is less harmful than smoking tobacco and, as this report emphasises, can help people to stop smoking. The long- term effects of e-cigarettes are unknown but the long-term harms of tobacco are indisputable.

Support from stop smoking services remain the most effective way to help people quit for good. Services can help people find the tool that works for them, e-cigarette or otherwise, and give them the best chance of reducing their risk from tobacco.

23 February 2021

The above information is reprinted with kind permission from Public Health England and UK Health Security Agency.
© Crown copyright 2022
This information is licensed under the Open Government Licence v3.0
To view this licence, visit http://www.nationalarchives.gov.uk/doc/open-government-licence/

www.gov.uk

Vape users warned about potential explosions or fire if they use wrong batteries

'The devices [can] result in serious injury and also death,' says product safety lead officer Mark Gardiner.

By Sophie Gallagher

Vape and e-cigarette users have been warned by the government to only use batteries or charging devices that are recommended by manufacturers to avoid accidents.

The Office for Product Safety and Standards (OPSS) and Chartered Trading Standards Institute (CTSI) say that failure to do so could potentially cause fire risks or even explosions.

The warning comes as the number of people using the smoking-devices grows rapidly: between 5.4 and 6.2 per cent of all adults in Britain now use a vape or e-cigarette.

This equates to between 14.9 and 18.5 per cent of current smokers.

The campaign has been launched following a series of incidents that have seen devices catch fire, including one that exploded in a teenager's mouth leaving him with shattered teeth.

Another incident in 2018 saw a man in Florida die when his vape exploded and gave him 80 per cent body burns.

The London Fire Brigade said they attend an average of 24 fires per week caused by batteries, cables or chargers.

Many vapes and e-cigarettes are powered by 18650-style batteries, which are slightly larger than the common AA battery.

The OPSS and CTSI have said that these batteries are widely available to purchase but that consumers should be vigilant about checking the voltages.

They have also urged users to solely use the charger supplied with the device, and not a phone charger or other equivalent.

Product safety lead officer at CTSI Mark Gardiner said: 'There have been numerous reports of hazardous failure modes of the devices containing these batteries, resulting in serious injury and also death.

'Where products are supplied with the battery already installed, the manufacturer of this device has generally added a battery management system to ensure safe charging and discharging.'

Gardiner said that problems can arise when 'unsuitable batteries' are either used by the retailer before the point of sale or consumers put in an unsuitable replacement without realising.

Both the London Fire Brigade and OPSS have also said vape and e-cigarette users should not charge devices overnight.

'It's important when replacing a battery that you check what type of battery you have and if manufacturers say it is safe for vape use,' added Gardiner.

The OPSS also advised that vape and e-cigarette users should unplug the device when it is fully charged and keep spare batteries away from metal items which could cause a short circuit.

17 February 2020

The above information is reprinted with kind permission from *The Independent*.
© independent.co.uk 2022

www.independent.co.uk

WHO warning on vaping draws harsh response from U.K. researchers

Risks and benefits of e-cigarettes fiercely disputed.

By Jennifer Couzin-Frankel

New warnings about vaping issued this week by the World Health Organization have prompted strong pushback from public health experts in the United Kingdom, who charged that WHO was spreading 'blatant misinformation' about the potential risks and benefits of e-cigarettes.

The pointed exchange comes amid growing controversy over the value of e-cigarettes, and how to weigh their role as a smoking cessation tool against their potential harms, especially among young people for whom vaping has soared in popularity. The statements align with others made by U.K. public health officials in recent months, which have generally supported vaping as a useful alternative to traditional cigarettes. In contrast, WHO's cautions about vaping echo those voiced by the U.S. Centers for Disease Control and Prevention and some U.S. scientists, who are expressing alarm over both known and still-uncertain hazards from vaping. After an outbreak of severe lung disease that's still being investigated and is linked to THC-containing e-cigarettes, CDC now recommends that e-cigarettes of all kinds 'never be used by youths.'

In a document released Monday, WHO expressed reservations about the value of e-cigarettes and grave concerns about their risks. The organization stated 'there is no doubt' that e-cigarettes 'are harmful to health and are not safe, but it is too early to provide a clear answer on the long-term impact of using them or being exposed to them.' WHO also suggested 'there is not enough evidence to support the use of these products for smoking cessation,' and urged smokers looking to quit to try nicotine patches or gum, or other tools such as hotlines that counsel smokers.

The U.K. response was harsh. 'The WHO has a history of anti-vaping activism that is damaging their reputation. This document is particularly malign,' Peter Hajek, who directs the Tobacco Dependence Research Unit at Queen Mary University of London, wrote in a statement released today by the U.K. Science Media Centre.

'There is no evidence that vaping is 'highly addictive,'' he said. 'Less than 1% of non-smokers become regular vapers. Vaping does not lead young people to smoking - smoking among young people is at [an] all-time low. … There is clear evidence that e-cigarettes help smokers quit,' Hajek continued.

E-cigarettes are 'clearly less harmful' than tobacco, said John Britton, director of the UK Centre for Tobacco & Alcohol Studies and a consultant in respiratory medicine at the University of Nottingham, in similarly critical comments. 'WHO misrepresents the available scientific evidence,' he charged. Public Health England maintains that vaping is 'at least 95% less harmful than smoking cigarettes.'

Earlier this month, a team of six experts disputed that 95% claim in a publication in the American Journal of Public Health. Led by Thomas Eissenberg, a psychologist at Virginia Commonwealth University who co-directs the Center for the Study of Tobacco Products and serves as a paid consultant in litigation against the tobacco and e-cigarette industries, the authors suggested there is an 'accumulation of evidence of potential harm' from e-cigarettes and 'growing evidence that e-cigarette use is associated with subsequent cigarette smoking.' Although tobacco use among U.S. middle and high school students has dropped, a 2017 study in JAMA Pediatrics reported that across seven studies that examined initiation of smoking in teenagers and young adults, those who had used e-cigarettes had a 23% chance of starting to smoke, compared with a 7% chance when there was no e-cigarette use.

The short- and long-term risks of e-cigarettes continue to be investigated; whereas many believe the products are lower risk than cigarettes, others say the jury is still out. Studies in animals and people are now exploring whether e-cigarettes pose chronic risks to the lungs and cardiovascular system.

The question of whether e-cigarettes help smokers quit, and at what cost, remains controversial. Tobacco kills more than 8 million people a year worldwide, and many smokers have shared publicly that e-cigarettes helped them. A randomized trial run by Hajek and others reported a year ago in The New England Journal of Medicine that e-cigarettes were more effective tools than nicotine replacement therapy when it came to helping smokers quit. As happens often in the vaping field, however, the data came under scrutiny: Subsequent letters to the journal noted, among other concerns, that 40% of the 438 participants assigned to e-cigarettes as a quitting tool were still using them after 1 year, and one-quarter of those in the e-cigarette group wound up becoming 'dual users,' meaning they both vaped and smoked.

The dispute is unlikely to be resolved soon. But for WHO, the downside of e-cigarettes clearly outweighs their benefits. E-cigarettes 'are currently banned in over 30 countries worldwide,' the group shared this week, 'with more and more countries considering bans to protect young people.'

22 January 2020

The above information is from *Science* reprinted with permission from AAAS.
©2022 American Association for the Advancement of Science.

www.science.org

A damning review of e-cigarettes shows vaping leads to smoking, the opposite of what supporters claim

An article from *The Conversation*.

By Paul Grogan, Adjunct Senior Lecturer, The Daffodil Centre, University of Sydney & Guy Marks, Professor of Respiratory Medicine, South Western Sydney Clinical School, UNSW Sydney

A major review on the health effects of e-cigarettes reflects what public health advocates have feared – escalating use of e-cigarettes in school-aged children, early warning signs of increased smoking rates in young Australians, and direct health harms of vaping in all ages.

The review, which was released today, was commissioned by the federal health department and conducted by researchers at the Australian National University.

Overall, it found the health risks from e-cigarettes significantly outweighed any potential benefits.

The review should silence lobbyists, who have long used data selectively to promote the sale of e-cigarettes. This is despite the fact previous reports, none as comprehensive and rigorous as this latest review, have delivered similar findings.

What does the review tell us?

The review looked at the evidence behind the health impacts of e-cigarettes or 'vapes' – a diverse group of devices that aerosolise a liquid for inhalation. These are touted as a safer alternative to cigarettes and an aid to quit smoking.

The review found conclusive clinical evidence e-cigarettes cause acute (short-term) lung injury, poisoning, burns, seizures, and their use leads to addiction. They also cause less serious harms, such as throat irritation and nausea.

Evidence e-cigarettes produce airborne particles in indoor environments (potentially harming non-users) was also conclusive.

Among evidence ranked as strong, the review confirms what has worried tobacco control experts since patterns of e-cigarette use first emerged.

People who have never smoked or are non-smokers are three times as likely to smoke if they use e-cigarettes, compared with people who have never used e-cigarettes.

This is a dream for tobacco companies and their retail allies.

Weighing up the harms and the benefits

The review found limited evidence e-cigarettes assist individuals to stop smoking. But this is no stronger than evidence showing e-cigarette use might also cause former smokers to relapse and revert to tobacco.

There is no conclusive or strong evidence in the review for any beneficial outcome from e-cigarettes.

E-cigarettes might help some individuals stop smoking. So they should only be available via a prescription from authorised medical professionals trained in helping people to quit. Any access beyond this risks serious harm for no benefit.

Young people are vaping

Australian Institute of Health and Welfare data show the age group most likely to use e-cigarettes in their lifetime are 18 to 24-year-olds. This has risen from 19.2% in 2016 to 26.1% in 2019.

Of e-cigarette users who identify as smokers, the second largest user group is 14 to 17- year-olds. Dual use is starting young, from the limited Australian Institute of Health and Welfare data we have.

The Australian Institute of Health and Welfare data precedes increasingly visible use of e-cigarettes in Australian schools, reported in the media.

The review also shows young males are the leading e-cigarette user group by age and sex. Australian males aged 18-24 are also the only age group which, on the latest Australian Institute of Health and Welfare data, are smoking at greater rates than they were three years earlier.

We need to limit access

Whatever benefits might be delivered by e-cigarettes, such as helping people to quit smoking, would, according to the review, be modest compared with the harms they are likely to cause.

Unfortunately, public policy on the regulation of e-cigarettes is at risk of influence from powerful commercial interests. In the interests of public health, these forces must be resisted.

What should governments do?

Federal, state and territory governments have enacted policies aimed at providing e-cigarette access to individuals who might benefit from them to quit smoking, while protecting everyone else.

But the evidence on how widely e-cigarettes are used shows these policies need to be more tightly enforced.

It's still easy to buy e-cigarettes online, they are available without prescription from petrol stations, tobacconists, speciality 'vape' stores and are on-sold by entrepreneurs – all of them acting unlawfully. Heavy fines will end their cash incentive.

The review shows the risks to public health posed by e-cigarettes will only grow unless governments enforce their laws.

This is to protect young Australians from becoming the first generation since trend data was collected to smoke and use nicotine at higher rates than their predecessors.

6 April 2022

The above information is reprinted with kind permission from The Conversation.
© 2010-2022, The Conversation Trust (UK) Limited

www.theconversation.com

E-cigarettes could be prescribed on the NHS in world first

England could be the first country in the world to prescribe medicinally licensed e-cigarettes to help reduce smoking rates.

- Medical regulator to work with manufacturers to assess safety and effectiveness of products
- Move supports government ambition for England to be smoke-free by 2030 and to reduce stark health disparities in smoking rates

E-cigarettes could be prescribed on the NHS in England to help people stop smoking tobacco products, as Health and Social Care Secretary Sajid Javid welcomed the latest step forward in the licensing process for manufacturers.

The Medicines and Healthcare products Regulatory Agency (MHRA) is publishing updated guidance that paves the way for medicinally licensed e-cigarette products to be prescribed for tobacco smokers who wish to quit smoking.

Manufacturers can approach the MHRA to submit their products to go through the same regulatory approvals process as other medicines available on the health service.

This could mean England becomes the first country in the world to prescribe e-cigarettes licensed as a medical product.

If a product receives MHRA approval, clinicians could then decide on a case-by-case basis whether it would be appropriate to prescribe an e-cigarette to NHS patients to help them quit smoking. It remains the case that non-smokers and children are strongly advised against using e-cigarettes.

E-cigarettes contain nicotine and are not risk free, but expert reviews from the UK and US have been clear that the regulated e-cigarettes are less harmful than smoking. A medicinally licensed e-cigarette would have to pass even more rigorous safety checks.

Smoking remains the leading preventable cause of premature death and while rates are at record low levels in the UK, there are still around 6.1 million smokers in England. There are also stark differences in rates across the country, with smoking rates in Blackpool (23.4%) and Kingston upon Hull (22.2%) poles apart from rates in wealthier areas such as Richmond upon Thames (8%).

E-cigarettes were the most popular aid used by smokers trying to quit in England in 2020. E-cigarettes have been shown to be highly effective in supporting those trying to quit, with 27.2% of smokers using them compared with 18.2% using nicotine replacement therapy products such as patches and gum.

Some of the highest success rates of those trying to quit smoking are among people using an e-cigarette to kick their addiction alongside local Stop Smoking services, with up to 68% successfully quitting in 2020 to 2021.

Health and Social Care Secretary Sajid Javid said:

> **'This country continues to be a global leader on healthcare, whether it's our COVID-19 vaccine roll-out saving lives or our innovative public health measures reducing people's risk of serious illness.**
>
> **Opening the door to a licensed e-cigarette prescribed on the NHS has the potential to tackle the stark disparities in smoking rates across the country, helping people stop smoking wherever they live and whatever their background.'**

Almost 64,000 people died from smoking in England in 2019 and the Office for Health Improvement and Disparities (OHID) is supporting efforts to level up public health and ensure communities across the country have equal health outcomes.

Reducing health disparities – including in smoking rates – and keeping people in better health for longer is good for the individual, families, society, the economy and NHS. To achieve this overall ambition, OHID will work collaboratively at national, regional and local levels as well as with the NHS, academia, the third sector, scientists, researchers and industry.

The government will soon publish a new Tobacco Control Plan which will set out the roadmap for achieving a smoke-free England by 2030.

The NHS can only prescribe e-cigarettes when the National Institute for Health and Care Excellence (NICE) recommends them for use.

29 October 2021

The above information is reprinted with kind permission from Department of Health & Social Care and Office for Health Improvement and Disparities.
© Crown copyright 2022
This information is licensed under the Open Government Licence v3.0
To view this licence, visit http://www.nationalarchives.gov.uk/doc/open-government-licence/

www.gov.uk

Chapter 3: Quitting

The benefits of stopping smoking

Across the UK, people are putting down the cigarettes and taking up the challenge of Stoptober. This is when, during October, people are encouraged to not smoke for 28 days. Studies have shown that if you're able to go 28 days without a cigarette, you are five times more likely to quit for good.

When you first start thinking about quitting smoking, it can be easy to get overwhelmed. It can feel like such a big challenge to take on and you may not feel like you're up to it.

However, rather than focus on the challenges you may face giving up smoking, you can remind yourself of all the things you can gain during the process. From improving your heart and lungs to having more energy and money. We've put together a list of how you could benefit from stopping smoking.

Every day you don't smoke, you are taking a further step into living a healthier lifestyle. If you're looking for some motivation into taking that first step with your stop smoking journey, then you're in the right place.

Lung health & immunity

Smoking affects your lung function and immunity. We've all come to realise just how important both of these things are during the past 18 months. After quitting, the cilia (tiny hairs) in your lungs can start to repair and clear out mucus and dirt. This allows your body to fight infections better.

It doesn't take long for your body to start feeling these benefits. After just 48 hours, all carbon monoxide will be flushed out of your system. After 72 hours, you'll be breathing easier. Your bronchial tubes (the airways in your lungs) will have started to relax. You'll find your energy levels increasing. You'll notice an improved sense of taste and smell.

Healthy heart

Stopping smoking doesn't just help your lungs and immune system, it also helps your heart. Within hours of quitting, your heart rate will return to normal. During the first three months, blood will be pumping through your heart and muscles better because your circulation will have improved. After quitting smoking for a whole year, your risk of having a heart attack will have halved compared to a smoker's.

Mental health

While there are plenty of physical benefits to talk about, did you know that stopping smoking boosts your mental health and well-being? It's a common belief that smoking helps you relax, but this is not true. Smoking makes you feel more tense and anxious. This is because it confuses the chemicals in your brain. When you don't have a cigarette for a while, you may notice you start to feel irritable and anxious. You associate your mood improving with having a cigarette, when the smoking itself is impacting your mood.

Studies have shown that when people stop smoking: anxiety and depression levels lower, mood improves, and in some cases people can lower their medication used to treat their mental health problems.

Family

Making the decision to stop smoking will not only benefit you but also your family. You can make a positive impact on your children, or grandchildren. Did you know that children are three times more likely to smoke if their parents or grandparents smoke too? By changing your habits now, you can help them in the future.

Finances

Quitting smoking can benefit your health and those around you. However, it can also benefit your bank account. On average, most people who quit smoking save around £250 per month. When a pack costs approximately £10, you can see how quickly this adds up.

If you're thinking about quitting smoking, remember that you don't have to do it alone. If you choose to use a stop smoking treatment, along with having expert support from your local stop smoking service, you will be 3 times more likely to quit successfully.

7 October 2021

The above information is reprinted with kind permission from *MoreLife*
© MoreLife 2022

www.more-life.co.uk

Quitting smoking is linked to improved mental health, research finds

People who stop smoking may experience improvements in their mental health such as reductions in anxiety and depression symptoms, finds research carried out in collaboration with the University of Birmingham.

People who stop smoking may experience improvements in their mental health such as reductions in anxiety and depression symptoms, finds research carried out in collaboration with the University of Birmingham.

Led by the University of Bath, in collaboration with the Universities of Birmingham, Oxford and New York, the Cochrane Review found that those who quit smoking are not likely to experience a worsening in their mood long-term, whether they have a mental health condition or not.

Published to coincide with No Smoking Day 2021, the research also found that people's social relationships are unlikely to suffer if they give up smoking.

Smoking is the world's leading cause of preventable illness and death. One in every two people who smoke will die of a smoking-related disease unless they quit. However, some people still believe that smoking reduces stress and other mental health symptoms, and that quitting might exacerbate mental health problems. Some people who smoke also worry that stopping might have a negative impact on their social lives and friendships.

The review, which summarises evidence from 102 observational studies involving nearly 170,000 people, found that people who stopped smoking for at least six weeks experienced less depression, anxiety, and stress, than people who continued to smoke. People who quit also experienced more positive feelings and better psychological wellbeing, and it is possible that stopping smoking may be associated with a small improvement in social wellbeing.

Lead author Dr Gemma Taylor, of the Addiction & Mental Health Group at the University of Bath, said: 'Smokers often believe that cigarettes are the crutch they need when they feel low, but there is good reason to think that smoking is actually making them feel worse.

'The daily cycle of waking up with cravings, satisfying the cravings through smoking only to be back wanting another cigarette within hours has an understandable impact on how people feel.

'But get past the withdrawal that many smokers feel when they stop, and better mental health is on the other side.

'From our evidence we see that the link between smoking cessation and mood seem to be similar in a range of people, and most crucially, there is no evidence that people with mental health conditions will experience a worsening of their health if they stop smoking.'

Dr Amanda Farley, Lecturer in Public Health and Epidemiology at the University of Birmingham, said: 'Cochrane reviews bring together all the latest research evidence using systematic and rigorous methods to answer a specific question.

'Our review finding that, after a short withdrawal period, mental health is not worse in those who quit smoking and instead is linked with improved mood is good news for smokers, and may help to address some myths that smoking helps mental health.'

The review authors combined the results from 63 studies that measured changes in mental health symptoms in people who stopped smoking with changes occurring in people who continued to smoke. They also combined results from 10 studies that measured how many people developed a mental health disorder during the study. The studies involved a wide range of people, including people with prior mental health conditions and people with long-term physical illnesses. The length of time the studies followed people varied from six weeks to up to six years.

The new research comes as Public Health England has published data that shows smokers have poorer mental well-being than non-smokers. The data shows that in 2019, 1.6 million smokers had high levels of anxiety. As anxiety increased for the whole population in 2020 as a result of COVID-19, 2.4 million smokers reported high levels of anxiety - an increase of 50%. Smokers reporting low levels of happiness also rose, from 900,000 in 2019, to 1.3 million in 2020.

Deborah Arnott, Chief Executive of Action on Smoking and Health, said: 'After the year we've all had, some smokers might feel now is not the time to stop.

'The opposite is true, put smoking behind you and a brighter future beckons. Using nicotine replacement, whether patches, gum or vapes, can help deal with any withdrawal symptoms, which last at most a matter of weeks. Be confident that once you've put smoking behind you not only will you be healthier and wealthier but feel happier too.'

10 March 2021

The above information is reprinted with kind permission from University of Birmingham
© University of Birmingham 2021

www.birmingham.ac.uk

Smoking and pregnancy: financial incentives can double abstinence rates

An article from *The Conversation*.

By Léontine Goldzahl, Professeur Associé, EDHEC Business School, Florence Jusot, Professeure en Sciences Economiques, Université Paris Dauphine – PSL, Ivan Berlin, MCU-PH, Hôpital Pitié-Salpêtrière (AP-HP) – Département de pharmacologie, Sorbonne Université, Faculté de médecine – CESP-INSERM 1018, Sorbonne Université & Noémi Berlin, Chargée de recherche CNRS, laboratoire EconomiX, Université Paris Nanterre – Université Paris Lumières

The adverse effects of maternal smoking during pregnancy are well known. Pregnant women who smoke are at higher risk of miscarriage, fetal death, prematurity and low birth weight. Smoking during pregnancy also affects the health of the child, as it increases the risk of asthma, psychiatric disorders, and obesity.

Even if pregnant women are aware of the health risks, they may continue to smoke. Nicotine replacement therapies, such as patches, appear to be less effective for pregnant women than in the general smoking population. Other support methods, such as counselling by specialists or cognitive-behavioural therapy, do not work well for pregnant smokers. Thus, 25% pregnant women smoked at least occasionally (and 22% were daily smokers) in France in 2017.

This long-standing trend is too high given the health risks for the newborns and the mothers. It is therefore necessary to explore other therapeutic avenues to help pregnant smokers quit. Economic theory indicates that a financial reward can lead to a change in health behaviour.

Why would providing financial rewards change a health behaviour?

Although smoking is above all an addiction, smoking cessation, like any other decision, is the result of a trade-off between the costs such as the loss of the satisfaction derived from smoking and efforts required to stop, and the benefits such as the money saved from not buying cigarettes and the perception of health improvement due to smoking cessation.

Providing financial rewards to quitters could compensate for their efforts and loss of satisfaction derived from smoking. The financial rewards would affect the trade-off such that the benefits of quitting would outweigh the costs.

Would it then be effective to offer a financial reward to help pregnant women quit smoking? To find out, we set up a randomised trial involving 460 pregnant women in 18 maternity wards in France. Our study, published in the British Medical Journal, aimed to test the effectiveness of conditional financial incentives for smoking cessation in pregnant smokers.

The participants, all in their first trimester of pregnancy, were randomly assigned, into two groups of equal size: a financial incentives group receiving financial incentives conditional on abstinence and a control group that did not. Monthly face-to-face visits were planned that included routine medical and smoking cessation counselling up to the end of the pregnancy. At each visit, the pregnant women met with health care professionals specifically trained for smoking cessation skills.

The participants' smoking abstinence was assessed by self-report of smoking, and by a test measuring carbon monoxide level in the expired air, a standard measure of smoke exposure. At each visit, participants of the financial incentives group received vouchers whose amount depended on their current abstinence, and on their past abstinence. The more times they were abstinent, the larger was the amount of financial rewards. The maximum amount that could be earned in the study was 520 euros. Each 20 € voucher could be redeemed in many shops (including groceries, childcare equipment, etc.) but they could not be used to purchase tobacco or alcohol.

The financial incentives schedule was specifically designed to encourage continuous abstinence throughout pregnancy, as only continuous abstinence might have a major impact on the newborn's health.

Financial incentives doubled the number of pregnant women who stopped smoking

Financial incentives conditional on abstinence helped women quit smoking throughout their pregnancy and improved some major birth characteristics. With no financial incentives, 7.42% of the participants quit smoking throughout their pregnancy. Among those who benefited from financial incentives, this rate reached 16.45%. Hence, financial incentives were associated with doubling continuous smoking abstinence rate. The figure above shows that smoking abstinence was also systematically higher at each medical visit in the group that received financial incentives.

These results translate into better health outcomes for the newborns. Newborns were less likely to have a low birth weight, a known predictor of perinatal and infant adverse health events. Poor neonatal outcomes (transfer to neonatal unit, convulsion, malformation, and deaths) decreased by 5.3 percentage points between newborns of participants who were in the financial incentives group compared to those in the control group. The intervention had no effect on prematurity.

Benefits long after pregnancy

Would public health authorities implement financial incentives into the health care routine of pregnant smokers? Our results show that providing financial incentives conditional on abstinence is effective in increasing smoking cessation rate throughout the pregnancy and improve birth characteristics. But the evaluation of the impact of this measure should not be limited to this period of life. Healthier newborns may also become healthier children then adults.

Before choosing to implement such an unusual policy, public decision-makers may ask themselves how it would be perceived by the general population. We had precisely evaluated its acceptability before carrying out our study, by surveying a representative sample of the French population. More than 50% of respondents were in favor of this type of policy. As other studies from other countries have shown that acceptability of financial incentives increases when proof of effectiveness is provided, we are confident that this policy could be widely accepted in France.

10 March 2022

The above information is reprinted with kind permission from The Conversation
© 2010-2022, The Conversation Trust (UK) Limited

www.theconversation.com

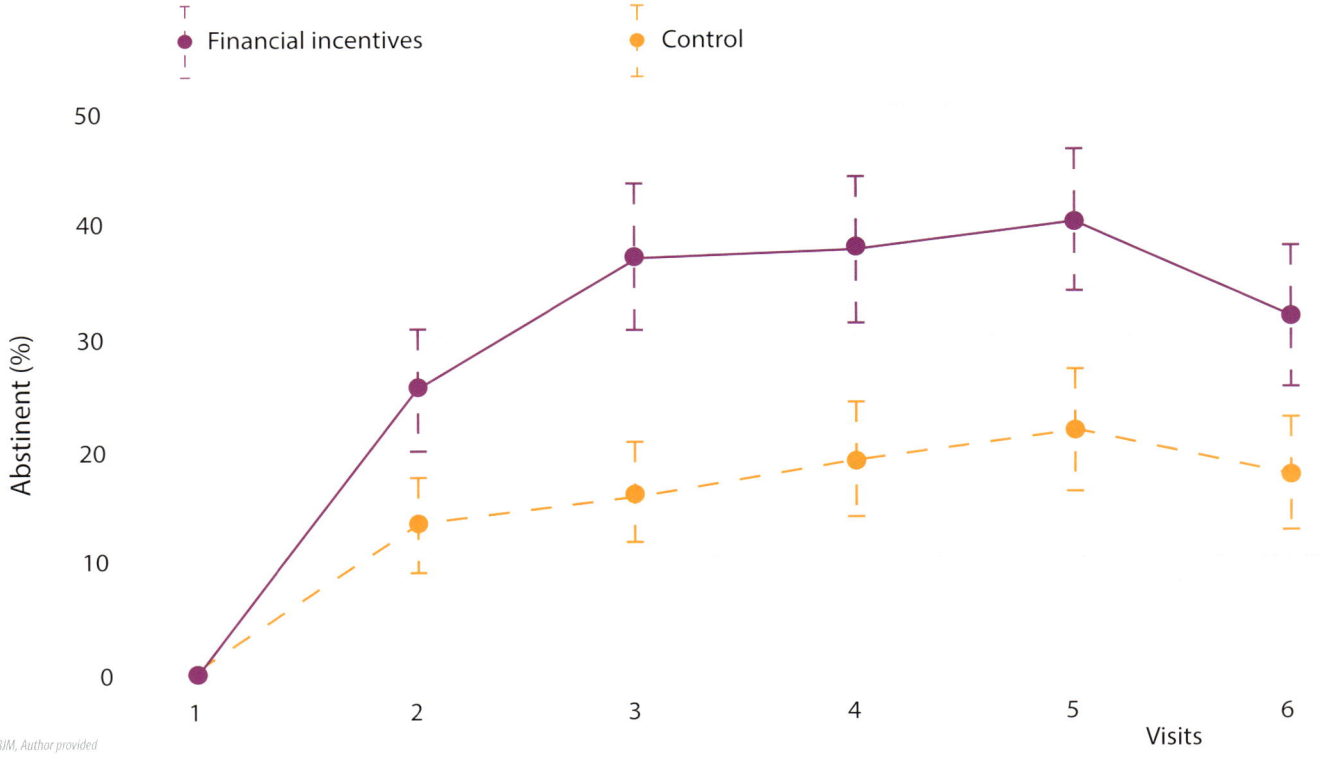

Financial incentives doubled the number of pregant women who stopped smoking

Smoke-free England by 2030: on track or unrealistic?

Rates of smoking in Britain are among the lowest in Europe. Despite this, smoking is still a major cause of early death. Smoking rates remain tied to economic factors, with research showing as personal income increases, the likelihood of smoking decreases. This article looks at the statistics and research around smoking. It also considers the Government's ambition of going smoke-free by 2030 in England, and 2034 in Scotland.

By Philip Lewis

In July 2019, the Government stated its ambition of going 'smoke-free' by 2030 in England. In Scotland, the target is 2034, while Northern Ireland and Wales have not yet set a date. In practice, 'smoke-free' involves reaching 5% average adult smoking prevalence. The Government has acknowledged that this goal will be 'extremely challenging' to achieve. Over the last 35 years, smoking rates in Britain have halved. According to Cancer Research UK, currently around 15% of UK adults smoke cigarettes. This is among the lowest rate in Europe.

A February 2020 report from Cancer Research UK states that to reach the 5% target by 2030, the pace of change needs to be '40% faster' than is currently predicted.

Smoking: a habit in decline

Smoking was banned in enclosed public places in Scotland in 2006, and the rest of the UK in 2007. Also in 2007, the minimum age for purchasing tobacco rose from 16 to 18 in Scotland, England and Wales. Plain packaging for cigarettes was introduced in 2016, following an independent review. The review concluded that:

'There is sufficient evidence that the introduction of standardised packaging as part of a comprehensive policy of tobacco control measures would be very likely over time to contribute to a reduction in smoking prevalence, especially in children and young adults.'

A particular focus on preventing the uptake of smoking in children and young people has seen the proportion of children who smoke fall from 1 in 5 two decades ago, to 1 in 20 in 2018.

Despite this progress, in 2019 there were still nearly 7 million smokers in the UK. In 2017, 16% of all deaths in England were attributable to smoking.

Economic factors

Prevalence of smoking is strongly correlated with socio-economic status. Research suggests that as personal income increases, the likelihood of smoking decreases. In England, around 23% of those in routine or manual employment smoke, compared to around 9% of those in managerial and professional occupations. This gap has widened since 2012.

Hospital admissions attributable to smoking are significantly higher in economically deprived areas. In 2018, Blackpool, which ranks number one in local authority deprivation rankings, recorded the joint highest incidence of smoking related hospital admissions (2,900 per 100,000 population). In Wokingham, which ranks 316 out of 317 authorities in the deprivation rankings, this was 721 per 100,000.

Smoking prevalence is also higher among:

♦ unemployed people;

♦ those living with mental health conditions;

♦ people with no qualifications; and

♦ renters compared to property owners.

Action on Smoking and Health (ASH) have highlighted some causes of these disparities. A smoker whose 'socio-economic or psychosocial needs are unmet on a daily basis' may not prioritise quitting and may view smoking as a necessary everyday coping strategy for stress relief. In addition, children and young people exposed to adults smoking in their households are more likely to start smoking themselves, creating an inter-generational cycle of tobacco addiction.

The Government addressed these health inequalities in its 2017 'Tobacco Control Plan for England'. It states that Public Health England (PHE) will 'target support at those areas with high levels of smokers'. It also calls for local councils to:

'Identify the groups and areas with the highest smoking prevalence within their local communities and taking focused action aimed at making reductions in health inequalities caused by smoking in their population.'

How realistic is the 2030 target?

A group of charities, including ASH, the British Heart Foundation and Cancer Research UK, have published the 'Roadmap to a Smoke-Free 2030'. It states that if the Government is to meet the 2030 target, it must to commit to certain further measures. These include:

♦ legislating to force tobacco manufacturers to finance a smoke-free 2030 fund (sometimes known as the 'polluter pays' principle);

♦ ensuring universal access to support for smokers to quit, in both healthcare and community settings; and

- further policy consultations, including requiring retailers to have a licence to sell tobacco.

Cancer Research UK state that the combination of pharmacotherapy and behavioural support offered by local smoking cessation services is 'the most successful way to support smokers to stop'. Concern has been raised about the impact of public sector cuts on these services.

One of the major achievements of tobacco control over the last two decades has been a shift in social norms and public attitudes toward smoking. ASH state that it is vital this continues in communities and groups where smoking still carries levels of status and acceptability. It is possible that, if a targeted approach is not taken, then more affluent areas will reach smoke-free status over a decade before poorer communities.

Some groups have presented alternative viewpoints. The Institute of Economic Affairs argue that smoking 'results in a net saving for the Government of £19.8 billion'. The Adam Smith Institute have called for greater focus on the promotion of tobacco harm reduction products, such as e-cigarettes.

Dr Katrina Brown from Cancer Research UK states if the 2030 target is met, 3.4 million fewer people will be smoking in England compared with current rates. However, she also states that:

'Unless Government acts to make smoking rates fall faster, we're unlikely to reach the target.'

Recent data suggests that more than one million people have given up smoking since the beginning of the Covid-19 pandemic. Researchers at University College London have found that more people have quit in 2020 than in any year since 2007.

What's next?

On 13 July 2020, Baroness Northover tabled an amendment to the Business and Planning Bill, stating that:

'Pavement licences may only be granted by a local authority subject to the condition that smoking is prohibited.'

On 20 July 2020, Lord Faulkner of Worcester is to ask the Government about the 'objective of making England smoke-free by 2030'.

14 July 2020

The above information is reprinted with kind permission from UK Parliament
© UK Parliament 2022
This information is licensed under the Open Parliament Licence v3.0
To view this licence, visit https://www.parliament.uk/site-information/copyright-parliament/open-parliament-licence/

www.lordslibrary.parliament.uk

Stop smoking treatments

If you want to stop smoking, several different treatments are available from shops, pharmacies and on prescription to help you beat your addiction and reduce withdrawal symptoms.

The best treatment for you will depend on your personal preference, your age, whether you're pregnant or breastfeeding and any medical conditions you have. Speak to your GP or an NHS stop smoking adviser for advice.

Research has shown that all these methods can be effective. Importantly, evidence shows that they are most effective if used alongside support from an NHS stop smoking service.

Nicotine replacement therapy (NRT)

The main reason that people smoke is because they are addicted to nicotine.

NRT is a medication that provides you with a low level of nicotine, without the tar, carbon monoxide and other poisonous chemicals present in tobacco smoke.

It can help reduce unpleasant withdrawal effects, such as bad moods and cravings, which may occur when you stop smoking.

Where to get it and how to use it

NRT can be bought from pharmacies and some shops. It's also available on prescription from a doctor or NHS stop smoking service.

It's available as:

- skin patches
- chewing gum
- inhalators (which look like plastic cigarettes)
- tablets, oral strips and lozenges
- nasal and mouth spray

Patches release nicotine slowly. Some are worn all the time and some should be taken off at night. Inhalators, gum and sprays act more quickly and may be better for helping with cravings.

There's no evidence that any single type of NRT is more effective than another. But there is good evidence to show that using a combination of NRT is more effective than using a single product.

Often the best way to use NRT is to combine a patch with a faster acting form such as gum, inhalator or nasal spray.

Treatment with NRT usually lasts 8-12 weeks, before you gradually reduce the dose and eventually stop.

Who can use it

Most people are able to use NRT, including:

- adults and children over 12 years of age – although children under 18 should not use the lozenges without getting medical advice first
- pregnant women – your doctor may suggest NRT if they think it would help you quit; read more about stopping smoking in pregnancy
- breastfeeding women – your doctor can advise you how to do this safely

Always read the packet or leaflet before using NRT to check whether it's suitable for you.

Sometimes it may be advisable to get medical advice first, for example if you have kidney or liver problems, or you've recently had a heart attack or stroke.

Possible side effects

Side effects of NRT can include:

- skin irritation when using patches
- irritation of nose, throat or eyes when using a nasal spray
- difficulty sleeping (insomnia), sometimes with vivid dreams an upset stomach
- dizziness
- headaches

Any side effects are usually mild. But if they're particularly troublesome, contact your GP as the dose or type of NRT may need to be changed.

Varenicline (Champix)

Varenicline (brand name Champix) is not currently available. It has been withdrawn as a precaution because of an impurity found in the medicine. It's not yet known whether it will be available again in future.

Varenicline is a medicine that works in 2 ways. It reduces cravings for nicotine like NRT, but it also blocks the rewarding and reinforcing effects of smoking. It was only available on prescription.

Speak to your GP or NHS stop smoking adviser who will be able to recommend an alternative treatment.

Bupropion (Zyban)

Bupropion (brand name Zyban) is a medicine originally used to treat depression, but it has since been found to help people quit smoking.

It's not clear exactly how it works, but it's thought to have an effect on the parts of the brain involved in addictive behaviour.

Where to get it and how to use it

Bupropion is only available on prescription, so you'll usually need to see your GP or contact an NHS stop smoking service to get it.

It's taken as 1 to 2 tablets a day. You should start taking it a week or 2 before you try to quit.

A course of treatment usually lasts around 7 to 9 weeks.

Who can use it

Bupropion is safe for most people to take, although there are some situations when it's not recommended.

For example, it's not suitable for:

- children under 18 years of age
- women who are pregnant or breastfeeding
- people with epilepsy, bipolar disorder or eating disorders

Possible side effects

Side effects of bupropion can include:

- dry mouth
- difficulty sleeping (insomnia)
- headaches
- feeling and being sick
- constipation
- difficulty concentrating
- dizziness

Speak to your GP if you experience any troublesome side effects.

Serotonin syndrome

Serotonin syndrome is an uncommon, but potentially serious, set of side effects linked to some medicines.

Serotonin syndrome occurs when the levels of a chemical called serotonin in your brain become too high.

There is a risk of serotonin syndrome if you take other medicines such as:

- selective serotonin reuptake inhibitors (SSRIs)
- serotonin norepinephrine re-uptake inhibitors (SNRI)

Contact your GP or NHS 111 if you have any symptoms of serotonin syndrome, including:

- feeling or being sick
- diarrhoea
- increased heart rate
- feeling agitated

Go to 111.nhs.uk or call 111.

E-cigarettes

An e-cigarette is an electronic device that delivers nicotine in a vapour. This allows you to inhale nicotine without most of the harmful effects of smoking, as the vapour contains no tar or carbon monoxide.

Research has found that e-cigarettes can help you give up smoking, so you may want to try them rather than the medications listed above. As with other approaches, they're most effective if used with support from an NHS stop smoking service.

There are no e-cigarettes currently available on prescription.

For now, if you want to use an e-cigarette to help you quit, you'll have to buy one. Costs of e-cigarettes can vary, but generally they're much cheaper than cigarettes.

17 July 2019

The above information is reprinted with kind permission from the NHS.
© Crown copyright 2022
This information is licensed under the Open Government Licence v3.0
To view this licence, visit http://www.nationalarchives.gov.uk/doc/open-government-licence/

www.nhs.uk

Smoking banned in beer gardens by five councils across England

A growing number of councils are pushing for a ban on smoking outside venues.

By James Hockaday

Five local authorities in England have banned smoking outside cafes, pubs and restaurants, and others are considering doing the same.

These councils have started including the rules in their licensing agreements whenever hospitality venues apply to place tables and chairs outside.

It means people living under Newcastle City, Manchester City, Durham County, Northumberland County, or North Tyneside councils can't light up near outdoor seating areas — including in beer gardens.

Oxfordshire County Council is considering following suit, having announced its aim to go completely smoke-free by 2025. The move would see smoking banned not only near hospitality venues, but also outside workplaces.

A seventh local authority, Gateshead Council, does not have an official policy on outdoor smoking, but all of its licenses for pubs and restaurants and cafes now state that people must not smoke on the pavement.

The Government is pushing for the whole of England to achieve smoke-free status by 2030, meaning 5% or less of the population are smokers.

Attention has been drawn to smoking outside pubs as the Covid pandemic prompted a shift towards 'al fresco' drinking and dining.

There was a failed attempt to push an amendment through the House of Lords last year to ban smoking on pavements outside pubs.

Instead the Government compromised, announcing that venues must provide separate outdoor seating for smokers and non-smokers with clear signage.

But with a growing push to ban smoking outside venues completely, smokers' rights lobby groups are hitting back.

Simon Clark, director of Forest (Freedom Organisation for the Right to Enjoy Smoking Tobacco), said: 'It's no business of local councils if adults choose to smoke, and if they smoke outside during working hours that's a matter for them and their employer not the council.

'Nor should it be the role of councillors to force smokers to quit by extending the indoor smoking ban to any outdoor area where there is no risk to non-smokers.'

'The public will want local authorities to help local businesses bounce back from the impact of the pandemic. They will also be expected to focus on issues like employment and housing.

'Reducing smoking rates to meet some idealistic target is not a priority for most people and council policy should reflect that.'

Director of campaign group We Vape, Mark Oates, said: 'It now seems fashionable again to attack smokers instead of helping them, which is all these five councils are doing.

'They don't care about the individual smoker's health, they care about looking good. Smokers need to be educated in the alternatives, not treated like exiles.'

But Deborah Arnott, chief executive of Ash (Action on Smoking and Health), said most customers supported the idea of a pavement ban.

She told the Guardian: 'Our surveys show that two-thirds of the public want areas outside pubs and cafes to be smoke-free.

'It is not like this is not on anyone's radar. People complain a lot that if they go outside, they have to sit among smokers.'

England's chief medical officer, Professor Chris Whitty, recently told a conference more than 90,000 people died from tobacco related diseases in last year, compared with 75,000 from Covid-19.

He added: 'One in five people who die from cancer will die from [lung cancer]. The reason that people like me get very concerned and very upset about it is that this cancer is almost entirely caused for profit.'

3 June 2021

The above information is reprinted with kind permission from *Metro* & DMG Media Licensing.
© 2022 Associated Newspapers Limited

www.metro.co.uk

Countries share examples of how tobacco tax policies create win-wins for development, health and revenues

In 2018 only 38 countries, covering 14% of the global population, had sufficiently high tobacco taxes - which means taxing at least 75% of the cost of these health-harming products. By implementing proven policies like tobacco taxes, the costs created by the tobacco industry to local communities and nation can be avoidable. It is a win for population health, revenue and for development.

How The Gambia substantially reduced cigarette use using tobacco taxation

In 2012, prices of cigarettes in The Gambia were among the lowest in the African region. With WHO support, the country made a plan to raise the price of cigarettes. It worked so well the country went on to implement an even more ambitious plan for tobacco tax increases in the following years. As a result, revenues generated in 2018 were nearly three times as high compared to 2011. Meanwhile, cigarette importation was reduced by over 60%.

'The results of these plans exceeded our expectations,' said Mambury Njie, Honorable Minister of Finance and Economic Affairs of The Gambia. He said this convinced the country that increasing tobacco taxes is a win-win for bringing in more revenues while reducing demand.

'I hope that our experience in The Gambia will encourage other countries to embark on their own reforms, particularly at these COVID-19 pandemic times when the need for domestic resource mobilization that is health inclusive is paramount,' he said.

Sri Lanka uses regular increases on excise tax to decrease cigarette consumption

Sri Lanka now proudly meets the highest level of achievement of taxation for cigarettes, with taxes reaching 77% of the price of the most sold brand. In line with best-practices in the WHO Tobacco Taxation manual, Sri Lanka primarily relies on a specific excise tax, meaning a tax levied on selected products based on quantity, such as number of cigarettes or weight of tobacco.

It increased the tax at regular intervals to effectively decrease the affordability, and consumption of these deadly products. However, much still needs to be done to reduce the high prevalence of tobacco use in the country.

'We are certain that following more of the best practice outlined in the manual will help us address these persistent challenges and improve the health of the Sri Lankan population,' said Hon. Pavithra Devi Wanniarachchi, Minister of Health of Sri Lanka.

Increase in taxation of cigarettes in Colombia causes 34% drop in cigarette consumption

In 2016, Colombia had the second-cheapest cigarettes in the Western hemisphere, second only to Paraguay (a large producer of tobacco products).

As part of a larger fiscal reform in 2016, the specific tax rate for cigarettes was tripled from 2016 (COL$700 per pack) to 2018 (COL$2,100 per pack), with a 4% real increase per year after 2019.

Not only did cigarette consumption fall by 34% by 2018, but excise tax revenues, which are earmarked for funding of universal health coverage (UHC), almost doubled.

Therefore, the tobacco tax reform decreased tobacco consumption (along with associated death, disease, and costs); increased revenues; and contributed the financial sustainability of the UHC system. A win-win-win for Colombia.

Additionally, illicit trade in tobacco products was treated with the same level of sanctions as money laundering.

'There are ways to do things right and Colombia followed the example of those that had walked this road in the past, which is something you see reflected in the manual, those experiences that helped administrators design the right policies, design the right ways of administering these taxes and produce benefits such as the reduction in consumption of harmful products that improves the health of the populations and if you can use the additional revenues to also deliver better health, well that is an extra plus and an extra benefit,' said Dr Mauricio Cardenas, former Finance Minister and Public Credit, Colombia.

Oman's introduction of excise tax on tobacco led to substantial increases in tobacco prices that would effectively reduce tobacco use

After years of relying only on import duties for tobacco products, Oman introduced, as part of a joint decision from the Gulf Cooperation Council, a large excise tax in 2019 which led to large increases in prices making tobacco products less affordable.

According to the WHO estimates, the share of tax in the price of the most sold brand of cigarettes increased from 25% to almost 64% between 2018 and 2020 thanks to the introduction of the excise tax. The price of the most sold brand almost doubled from 1.2 to 2.2 Omani rials during that same period. We expect this will have a substantial impact on reducing tobacco use and uptake, especially the youth.

'I would like to [thank] the WHO for updating the technical manual on tobacco tax policy and administration, which is an important milestone for countries who wish to increase the effectiveness of their tax policies to reduce the burden of tobacco use. Focusing on tobacco taxes will also be very instrumental in the post-Covid-19 recovery efforts to raise more funds for health,' said Ahmed Mohammed Obaid Al Saidi, Minister of Health, Oman.

'Sin Tax' expands health coverage in the Philippines

The famous 2012 'Sin Tax' reform of the Philippines, which led to substantial reductions in tobacco use and increases in revenues used for UHC, has been very widely disseminated as a key success story on tobacco taxation. The Philippines has not stayed idle since.

The Philippines successfully foiled industry attempts to change the uniform tax structure for cigarettes under the Sin Tax Law of 2013. Cigarette taxes are now at their highest with increases of five pesos annually until 2023, and with automatic increases of 5% thereafter.

Through improved tax administration and stricter enforcement, the government penalized a domestic tobacco company for tax evasion in 2017; this resulted in the biggest tax settlement in Philippines history amounting to $US 600 million.

Excise taxes were also introduced on heated tobacco products and e-liquids used in electronic cigarettes. The structure for the excise tax on heated tobacco products is the same as for cigarettes, which is considered best practice. Moreover, unlike most countries, an excise tax is also imposed on those products' devices.

The tobacco and alcohol taxes earmarked for Universal Health Care were also redefined to be clearer and expanded to cover the sugar sweetened beverages tax. These generate more revenues for the health sector.

'The Philippine experience highlights what a strong political will can do to protect people from consuming products that have a deleterious impact on their health. It also shows how the government can overcome powerful vested interests in order to deliver long overdue reforms. We hope to further improve our tobacco tax policy and administration by observing the benchmarks and best practices contained in the manual that the World Health Organization brings to the public today,' said Carlos G. Dominguez III, Secretary of Finance, Philippines.

12 April 2021

The above information is reprinted with kind permission from *World Health Organization*.
©2022 WHO

www.who.int

Age restriction for buying cigarettes could be changed under new plan

Under-25s could be banned from buying cigarettes under plans being considered by a new anti-smoking tsar.

By James Hockaday

Javed Khan, former chief executive of children's charity Barnardo's, is leading an independent review on how to stop smoking in England.

The Government has set a target of the country going smoke-free by 2030, but with an estimated six million smokers there is still some way to go.

Tobacco is still the single largest cause of preventable death in England, with 64,000 people dying from smoking in 2019, according to the Office for National Statistics.

That's despite a steady drop in smoking over the past 20 years, with cigarette use falling from 15.8% in 2019 to 14.5% in 2020.

Late last year New Zealand took the step of banning anyone currently aged 14 and under from ever buying cigarettes – even after they become adults.

Now Mr Khan is considering whether to raise the minimum age to buy cigarettes to 25 in England in a bid to stop people picking up the habit.

He says the 2030 target would not be met if 'nothing different is done' to stamp out smoking. He is due to report his findings on April 22.

He also thinks the Government harness the power of social media to crack down on smoking like it did to get people vaccinated during the pandemic.

Mr Khan told *The Times:* 'Just look at the Covid experience, mass marketing has a big effect, it really works.

'The government went hell for leather, it made an enormous difference in vaccination rates.'

In his review, commissioned by Health Secretary Sajid Javid, Khan questioned whether the target of bringing smoking prevalence by 5% or less by 2030 goes far enough.

Up to 10% of pregnant women still smoke at the point of birth, with Mr Khan suggesting an escalation of pilot schemes offering women financial incentives to quit.

Last month Mr Khan asked the public what they thought on Twitter, writing: 'I want to hear your views and what we can do to support current smokers to quit, and to stop people taking up smoking.

'How do we stop people, especially children and young people, from starting smoking in the first place?

'Have you quit smoking for good? What worked? What do you think could work better?

'Have you ever used a Stop Smoking Service to quit smoking? Or spoken to your GP about it? What was your experience?'

Mr Khan added: 'I am very pleased to be leading this review into such an important area of public health.

'My independent findings will help highlight key interventions which can help the government achieve its ambitions to be smoke-free by 2030 and tackle health disparities.'

Many smokers know full well how dangerous their habit is and will simply ignore grave messages and grisly photos that are now plastered all over cigarette packets.

Robert West, Professor of Health Psychology and Director of Tobacco Studies at University College London, told Metro.co.uk how a safe and effective drug could prove a breakthrough in getting people to quit for good.

15 March 2022

The above information is reprinted with kind permission from *Metro* & DMG Media Licensing.
© 2022 Associated Newspapers Limited

www.metro.co.uk

How to help a friend quit smoking

The number of young people who took up smoking over lockdown has spiked, according to research

By Lisa Salmon

Although smoking has reduced massively over the last 70 years, worrying new figures show the boredom and stress of lockdown led to many more young people taking up the habit.

Research funded by Cancer Research UK found that during the first lockdown there was a 25 per cent increase in 18 to 34-year-olds who smoke, which translated into a rise of more than 652,000 young adults.

Bearing in mind that smoking rates had fallen from 82% in 1948 to 14.7 per cent in 2019, it's a concerning trend – as despite life returning to nearly normal as pandemic restrictions end, once nicotine addiction has kicked in, it won't be nearly as easy for new smokers to lose the cigarettes.

Action on Smoking and Health (Ash), says most smokers want to quit – in 2018 the Office for National Statistics (ONS) found 58.4 per cent of adult smokers wanted to stop – but they find it tough to give up without help.

Ash say only about 5 per cent of unaided quit attempts result in smokers giving up for good, but quitting support can increase the chances of success fourfold. And as well as official smoking cessation support like NHS Smokefree, the support of friends and family can be invaluable.

'With the worrying rise in young people smoking during the pandemic it would be great for people to look out for their friends,' says Hazel Cheeseman, Ash's deputy chief executive.

'Smokers are most likely to quit successfully if they get help. Long-term stopping smoking improves not just health but also wellbeing and has been estimated to have the same impact as antidepressants.'

Here's how to help a mate who's trying to quit:
Help them avoid emotional triggers

Many smokers will reach for a fag if they're feeling stressed, lonely, bored or anxious – or perhaps even when they're happy or satisfied, NHS Smokefree advises on their website. Let them know you're always there to chat if they need you, whatever the time.

Encourage them to exercise – and do it with them

As well as simply being good for you, physical activity can help take smokers' minds off cigarettes, and make them feel healthier and hopefully less likely to light up and cancel out their exercise efforts. Offer to exercise with them – it'll be good for you too, and it's much easier to motivate yourself if you're not exercising alone.

Help them identify and avoid situations that make them smoke

According to NHS Smokefree, there are many 'pattern triggers', like drinking alcohol or coffee, driving, or taking a break at work, can lead people to light up.

Help your friend identify what their triggers are, and devise a plan to avoid them, perhaps by thinking of ways they can change their routine, suggesting replacements like e-cigarettes or chewing gum, or buying them a stress ball so they've got something else to do with their hands.

Ash says research suggests electronic cigarettes are relatively harmless in comparison with smoking, and Cheeseman suggests: 'Encourage them to try alternative nicotine products like an e-cigarette to help manage the short-term cravings.'

Keep them busy

Encourage them to do things to take their mind off cigarettes, like going for a walk with you, going to the cinema (where they can't smoke), and helping them change their routine so they're not doing things where they would normally have smoked.

Quit yourself

If you smoke, try to quit with your mate, and if you don't smoke, make sure your social group knows your friend is trying to quit and ask them not to smoke when he or she is around. 'If you're a smoker yourself, get your friends to join you quitting – people who quit together are more likely to succeed,' stresses Cheeseman.

Help them focus on the positives

There's much more to gain than to lose when people quit smoking, so keep drumming it into your friend how well they're doing and what they're gaining, both health-wise and financially.

'Focusing on what you gain by stopping rather than what you lose is important,' says Cheeseman. 'Some people save up the money they would have spent on cigarettes to reward themselves, others join the gym and make the most of being able to breathe easier.'

Point them towards official help

As well as support from you, there's plenty of official help out there – smokers trying to quit can call the NHS helpline on 0300 123 1044 or download the NHS Smokefree app.

25 August 2021

The above information is reprinted with kind permission from *The Independent*.
© independent.co.uk 2022

www.independent.co.uk

Key Facts

- Globally the number of smokers has reached an all-time high of 1.1 billion, a study by The Lancet found in 2021. (page 1)

- Smoking killed almost 8 million people in 2019. (page 1)

- 89% of new smokers were addicted by the age of 25 but beyond that age were unlikely to start. (page 1)

- Smokers have an average life expectancy 10 years lower than those who have never smoked. (page 1)

- New economic analysis of national data commissioned by charity Action on Smoking and Health (ASH) published in 2022 shows the cost of smoking to society totals £17.04bn for England each year. This compares to £12.5bn under the previous estimate in 2019. (page 2)

- New analysis of national data commissioned by charity Action on Smoking and Health (ASH) published in 2022 finds that the proportion of smokers living in poverty is highest in the north and the midlands. (page 4)

- The average smoker is spending just under £2,000 a year on tobacco costing England smokers a total of £12 billion. (page 4)

- Lockdown due to the pandemic has reversed a 40 year decline in smoking. (page 6)

- Analysis by CRUK found that about 53,227 cancers a year are diagnosed among the poorest 20% of people in England as measured by the Office of National Statistics's index of multiple deprivation. Of those, an estimated 11,247 – 21% of the total – are caused directly by smoking, it said. (page 7)

- When smoked nicotine reaches the brain in about seven seconds. It is about the same when vaped, around 8-20 seconds. Nicotine reaches the central nervous system in about 3-5 minutes when tobacco is chewed. (page 8)

- Nicotine addiction, often described as nicotine dependence, is at least as addictive as heroin and cocaine per the US Surgeon General. (page 10)

- In a recent study, it was estimated that around one million UK workers are regularly exposed to second-hand smoke while they work. (page 13)

- Four out of 10 smokers and ex-smokers wrongly think nicotine causes most of the smoking-related cancers, when evidence shows nicotine actually carries minimal risk of harm to health. Although nicotine is the reason people become addicted to smoking, it is the thousands of other chemicals contained in cigarette smoke that cause almost all of the harm. (page 17)

- A study from UCL found that e-cigarettes helped an additional 50-70,000 smokers in England to quit in a single year. (page 17)

- Nicotine vaping products were the most popular aid (27.2%) used by smokers trying to quit in England in 2020. (page 18)

- Those using a vaping product as part of their quit attempt in local, stop smoking services have some of the highest quit-success rates – between 59.7% and 74% in 2019 to 2020. (page 18)

- Public Health England maintains that vaping is 'at least 95% less harmful than smoking cigarettes.' (page 21)

- Smoking remains the leading preventable cause of premature death and while rates are at record low levels in the UK, there are still around 6.1 million smokers in England. (page 24)

- Studies have shown that if you're able to go 28 days without a cigarette, you are five times more likely to quit for good. (page 25)

- Public Health England has published data that shows smokers have poorer mental well-being than non-smokers. The data shows that in 2019, 1.6 million smokers had high levels of anxiety. (page 27)

- Smoking was banned in enclosed public places in Scotland in 2006, and the rest of the UK in 2007. Also in 2007, the minimum age for purchasing tobacco rose from 16 to 18 in Scotland, England and Wales. Plain packaging for cigarettes was introduced in 2016. (page 30)

- The Government is pushing for the whole of England to achieve smoke-free status by 2030, meaning 5% or less of the population are smokers. (page 34)

- Research funded by Cancer Research UK found that during the first lockdown there was a 25 per cent increase in 18 to 34-year-olds who smoke, which translated into a rise of more than 652,000 young adults. (page 38)

Glossary

Addiction
A dependence on a substance which makes it very difficult to stop taking it. Addiction can be either physical, meaning the user's body has become dependent on the substance and will suffer negative symptoms if the substance is withdrawn, or psychological, meaning a user has no physical need to take a substance, but will experience strong cravings if it is withdrawn.

Cigarette
A paper tube filled with tobacco which is lit at one end and inhaled orally (smoked). There are many slang words for cigarettes, including fags, tabs, smokes and cigs/ciggies. Cigarettes can be bought pre-prepared or hand-rolled. Most modern cigarettes contain a spongy filter which reduces the amount of poisonous chemicals inhaled while smoking: however, a large part of these substances are still absorbed and smoking therefore poses a substantial health risk.

COPD (Chronic Obstructive Pulmonary Disorder)
A progressive disease, particularly common in smokers, affecting the lungs and making it increasingly difficult to breathe.

Dopamine
Dopamine is a chemical neurotransmitter produced in the brain. Nicotine stimulates the release of dopamine that triggers a 'feel-good' sensation.

E-cigarette
A battery-operated device that is typically designed to resemble a traditional cigarette and is used to inhale a usually nicotine-containing vapour.

E-liquid
The substance used inside an e-cigarette, sometimes known as 'vape juice', that creates the vapour and gives it its flavour and nicotine.

Nicotine
An addictive chemical compound found in the nightshade family of plants that makes up about 0.6-3.0% of dry weight of tobacco. It is the nicotine contained in tobacco which causes smokers to become addicted, and many will use Nicotine Replacement Therapy such as patches, gum or electronic cigarettes to help them deal with cravings while quitting.

Nicotine replacement therapy (NRT)
NRT is a smoking cessation aid. It provides low level nicotine without the tar, carbon monoxide and other toxic chemicals present in tobacco smoke. It is available over the counter or on prescription in patch, gum, lozenge, spray or inhaler form.

Secondhand smoke
Secondhand smoke is a mixture of the smoke from the burning end of a cigarette and the smoke exhaled by smokers. Exposure to to secondhand smoke is also known as passive smoking. People exposed to secondhand smoke face the same health risks as smokers themselves.

Smoking ban
The Health Act 2006, which came into force in England and Wales on 1 July 2007, made it illegal to smoke in all enclosed public places and enclosed work places (similar bans were already in place in other parts of the UK). This has led to much debate about the balance between public health and individual freedom.

Tar
A mixture of chemicals (including formaldehyde, arsenic and cyanide). About 70 per cent of the tar in a cigarette is left in smokers` lungs, causing a range of serious lung conditions.

Tobacco
Tobacco is a brown herb-like substance produced from the dried leaves of tobacco plants. The tobacco used in cigarettes contains many substances dangerous to the user when inhaled, including tar, which can cause lung cancer, and nicotine, which is highly addictive.

Vaping
The inhalation through the mouth of a vapour created by an e-cigarette or other vaping device.

Withdrawal
The symptoms that occur when a person stops taking a drug they are physically dependent on, making the person feel ill and suffer flu-like symptoms.

Activities

Brainstorming

- In small groups brainstorm what you know about smoking.

    - What are the health risks from smoking?
    - What are the harmful substances in tobacco?
    - Roughly how much is it to buy a packet of cigarettes in the UK today?
    - When was the ban on smoking in enclosed spaces introduced in the UK?
    - What are the side effects of using e-cigarettes and vaping?
    - What are e-liquids?
    - What are the benefits of stopping smoking?

Research

- Conduct a survey amongst your classmates and family members. How many of them smoke or vape. How many used to smoke tobacco and now vape instead? How many have stopped smoking or vaping altogether? Produce a graph to show your findings and share the result with your class.

- In pairs, do some research into using e-cigarettes and vaping. Find out how they affect health in comparison to smoking tobacco products.

- Do some research into smoking and cancer. What different types of cancers can be caused by smoking cigarettes and which is the most common?

- Conduct some online research into stopping smoking. Look up testimonies from ex-smokers and list the postive health benefits they say they now feel since quitting the habit.

Design

- In small groups produce a leaflet informing people about the different smoking cessation aids that are currently available to help them quit smoking.

- Imagine you work for an anti-smoking organisation. Create a poster with a striking image and a strong message warning people about the dangers of smoking.

- Choose one of the articles in this book and create an illustration that highlights its key message.

Oral

- Hold a class discussion about why you think some young people are attracted to using e-cigarettes or vapes, even though they have never been smokers. Do you think this might lead them to take up smoking cigarettes?

- In pairs create a presentation aimed at teenagers to discourage them from smoking or vaping. As well as the serious health risks, consider other reasons to quit or avoid smoking, such as:
    - the financial cost
    - the anti-social aspect
    - the impact on mood/mental health
    - the cosmetic effect, eg; stained teeth, bad breath

- In small groups, discuss why we don't know exactly how harmful vaping/e-cigarette use are, or if they are safer in the longer term than normal cigarettes.

Reading/writing

- Write a short paragraph explaining why smoking is so difficult to stop. Include information about nicotine and dopamine and the role they play in making it such an addictive habit.

- Imagine you are an agony aunt/uncle and have received an article from a child who is worried about their parents' smoking habits. They are scared their parents might develop a life-threatening condition or even die as a result of this. Write a suitable reply.

- Read the article *Smoking banned in beer gardens by five councils across England* (page 34). Write a letter to your local council asking if they plan to impose a similar ban where you live. Also suggest any other measures you can think of that could be introduced to help reduce smoking rates in your area.

- Choose one of the articles in this book and write a one-paragraph summary. List the three main points of the article.

- Choose two articles in this book and compare and contrast them. What differences do you notice?

Index

A
acetycholine 9
Action on Smoking and Health (ASH) 2–5, 19, 27, 30–31, 34, 38–39
addiction 8–10, 21, 33, 41
adrenaline 9
advertising 1
age restriction 37
anxiety, and smoking 8
asthma 14, 17

B
boys and men, smoking statistics 1
bupropion 33

C
cancer 1, 7, 19, 30–31, 34, 38
Cancer Research UK 7, 19, 30–31, 38
Chartered Trading Standards Institute (CTSI) 20
chronic obstructive pulmonary disease (COPD) 1, 41
cigarettes 1, 41
    advertising 1
    age restriction 37
    see also tobacco
cigars 8
Colombia, tobacco taxation 35–36
COVID-19
    impact on smoking 6, 18
    impact on vaping 18

D
death, from smoking 1, 3, 24
dopamine 8–9, 41

E
e-cigarettes 1, 8, 16–24, 33, 41
    see also vaping
e-liquids 36, 41

F
fire, smoking-related 3

G
Gambia, tobacco taxation 35
gender, and smoking 1
girls and women, smoking statistics 1

H
Health Act 2006 41
health inequalities 30
heart disease 1, 9, 16
Heart Research Institute (HRI) 12

L
life expectancy 1

M
maternal smoking 28–29
Medicines and Healthcare Products Regulatory Agency (MHRA) 24
mental health, and smoking 25–27

N
nicotine 8–11, 17, 41
nicotine replacement therapies (NRT) 18, 28, 32–33, 41

O
Office for Health Improvement and Disparities (OHID) 24
Office for Product Safety and Standards (OPSS) 20
Oman, tobacco taxation 36

P
packaging 30
passive vaping 17
Philippines, 'Sin Tax' 36
poverty, and smoking 4–5, 7, 30
pregnancy, and smoking 28–29

Q
quitting smoking 3, 17–18, 25–31, 37–39

S
second-hand smoke 14–15, 17, 41
serotonin syndrome 33
sleep apnoea 12–13
smoke-free targets 30–31, 34
smoking
    and addiction 8–10
    bans 14, 30, 34, 41
    costs of 2–3, 25
    deaths from 1, 3, 24
    and mental health 25–27
    quitting 3, 17–18, 25–31, 37–39
    rise in 6
    second-hand smoke 14–15, 17, 41
    see also vaping
snuff 8
Sri Lanka, tobacco taxation 35
Stoptober 25
stroke 1, 9, 14

T
tar 32, 41
tobacco 8, 41
    costs of 3
    industry 1, 3
    taxation 35–36
    see also cigarettes

V
vaping 8, 9, 16–24, 41
    see also e-cigarettes
varenicline 18, 33
ventilation 15
vitamin E acetate 16

W
Whitty, C. 34
withdrawal 9, 26–27, 32, 41
World Health Organization (WHO)
   on e-cigarettes 21
   on nicotine 9

Acknowledgements

The publisher is grateful for permission to reproduce the material in this book. While every care has been taken to trace and acknowledge copyright, the publisher tenders its apology for any accidental infringement or where copyright has proved untraceable. The publisher would be pleased to come to a suitable arrangement in any such case with the rightful owner.

The material reproduced in **issues** books is provided as an educational resource only. The views, opinions and information contained within reprinted material in **issues** books do not necessarily represent those of Independence Educational Publishers and its employees.

Images

Cover image courtesy of iStock. All other images courtesy Freepik, Pixabay & Unsplash.

Illustrations

Simon Kneebone: pages 19, 21 & 31. Angelo Madrid: pages 5, 27 & 32.

Additional acknowledgements

Page 35: Reprinted from: https://www.who.int/news-room/feature-stories/detail/countries-share-examples-of-how-tobacco-tax-policies-create-win-wins-for-development-health-and-revenues, *Countries share examples of how tobacco tax policies create win-wins for development, health and revenues,* Copyright (2021)

With thanks to the Independence team: Shelley Baldry, Klaudia Sommer and Jackie Staines. Contributing Editor: Tracy Biram.

Danielle Lobban

Cambridge, May 2022